Beat Generation

Jack Kerouac

ONEWORLD
CLASSICS

ONEWORLD CLASSICS LTD
London House
243-253 Lower Mortlake Road
Richmond
Surrey TW9 2LL
United Kingdom
www.oneworldclassics.com

Beat Generation first published in US in 2005 by Thunder's Mouth Press
Copyright © 2005 by Jack Kerouac and John Sampas, literary representative of
the Estate of John Kerouac
Introduction © A.M. Homes, 2005
All rights reserved

This edition first published by Oneworld Classics Limited in 2007
Notes and background material © Oneworld Classics Ltd, 2007

Printed in Great Britain by TJ International Ltd, Padstow, Cornwall

ISBN-13: 978-1-84749-007-0
ISBN-10: 1-84749-007-7

The Forest Stewardship Council (FSC) is an international, non-governmental
organisation dedicated to promoting re-sponsible management of the world's
forests. FSC operates a system of forest certification and product labelling
that allows consumers to identify wood and wood-based products from well-
managed forests. For more information about the FSC, please visit the website
at www.fsc-uk.org.

Contents

Jack Kerouac (1922–69)

A sketch drawing of
Jack Kerouac

Neal Cassady

The Kerouacs and family friend Armand Gauthier

Kerouac's birthplace in Lupine Road (left) and the house in Beaulieu Street where Gerard Kerouac died (right)

Poet Gregory Corso (back to camera), artist Larry Rivers, Jack Kerouac, composer David Amram and Allen Ginsberg taking a break during the 1959 filming of *Pull My Daisy*, an adaptation of *Beat Generation*

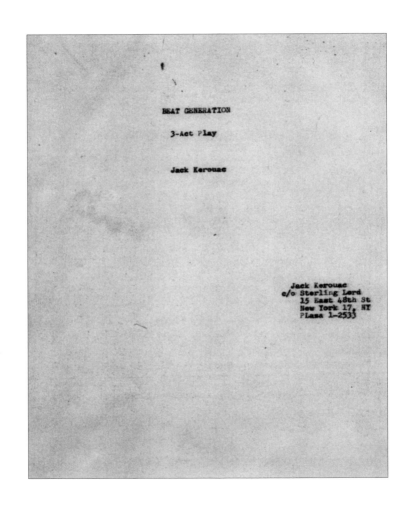

BEAT GENERATION

3-Act Play

Jack Kerouac

Jack Kerouac
c/o Sterling Lord
15 East 48th St
New York 17, NY
PLaza 1-2533

The title page of the original typescript
of *Beat Generation*

Introduction by A.M. Homes

IN ORDER TO TALK ABOUT IT you have to put it into some sort of a cultural context – it was 1957, Dwight D. Eisenhower was president, Richard M. Nixon vice-president, the Pulitzer Prize in drama went to Eugene O'Neill's *Long Day's Journey into Night* – no fiction award was given. *West Side Story* opened on Broadway, *Leave It to Beaver* premiered on television, and if you were going to the movies, chances are it was to see *The Bridge on the River Kwai*, *Twelve Angry Men* or *Peyton Place*. On the home front there was still a struggle to integrate the schools, while the Russians launched Sputnik I and the space age began. It was 1957, and Jack Kerouac's *On the Road* was published – other books that year included Bernard Malamud's *The Assistant*, James Agee's *A Death in the Family* and Noam Chomsky's *Syntactic Structures*.

At this point, Kerouac and his band of scribes were all about embracing and celebrating this "beat" life. Kerouac himself had already coined the term, according to some accounts as early as 1948, suggesting societal conventions were "beat", "tired", "worn out". Many have suggested that Kerouac's use of the term "Beat Generation" evolved from being a post-war reference to Hemingway's "Lost Generation" to a more positive label: the beats were enlightened, "beatific" ones – a nice confluence of the Buddhist and Catholic philosophies that were so important to Kerouac.

In 1957, Kerouac wasn't yet what he is today – a figure as or more dominant in contemporary culture as the faces on Mount Rushmore. In 1957, he still had the benefit of a certain anonymity – he was still, for the moment, the purest version of Jack Kerouac, not a personality, not a celebrity.

Unlike the World War II vets who came home, got married, moved to suburbia and fully embraced the American dream and the blossoming culture of more, more, more, keeping up with the Joneses and then some, the beat life was lived on the edges. Beats had nothing to lose and not far to fall. Holy men, mediators, anti-materialists, they were the exact opposite of "company men". Kerouac and his experimental fraternity aspired to something else – a kind of freedom. They wanted to soar, to fly, to move through time and space unfettered. They wanted to find spirituality and deliverance among the dispossessed. And they wanted to have a good time, win a few bucks on the horses, have some drinks and get laid. Compared to the average Joe they were wild – awe-inspiring and threatening.

Kerouac's style was not just philosophically bold; it was linguistic guerrilla warfare – a literary atom bomb smashing everything. On one side of him were the hyper-intellectual Beckett and Joyce. On the other, the anti-academic: Hemingway, Anderson and Dos Passos. Kerouac absorbed it all and went beyond.

In order to make sense of this play you have to keep it in perspective. It's now 2005, a line of Jack Kerouac clothing is about to be released, the manuscript of *On the Road* is on tour across America. A few months ago in a New Jersey warehouse this "new" play by Kerouac was discovered – three acts, written in 1957, and typed up by Kerouac's ever-loving mother, Gabrielle, also known as "Mémère".

The play was never produced – at the time there was a lot of interest but no action. In a letter Kerouac wrote he described his interest in theatre and film in this way:

> What I wanta do is redo the theatre and the cinema in America, give it a spontaneous dash, remove preconceptions of "situation" and let people rave on as they do in real life. That's what the play is: no plot in particular, no "meaning" in particular, just the way people are. Everything I write I do in the spirit where I imagine myself an angel returned to earth seeing it with sad eyes as it is.

The play *Beat Generation* marks a wonderful addition to the Kerouac oeuvre. It will be great fun to see what happens with it – I can easily imagine it being performed and each staging being incredibly different from the last – it's all about what you bring to it.

It is a play of its time – which is why context is important. In bits and pieces it is reminiscent of Tennessee Williams, Clifford Odets and a bit of Arthur Miller. But by comparison to those playwrights whose work is formal and well defined, this play is loose, unfettered; it is about juxtaposition, relation, words and ideas boucing off one another, riffing in a bebop scatter.

Beat Generation opens in the early morning in an apartment near the Bowery, with drinking – the reverie of the first glass. It is a man's world – these are working men, brakemen for the railroad, drinking men, who spend their day off betting on horses, men who swear by saying "durnit", men who have a girl waiting on them, warming their coffee – women's liberation never made it into Kerouac's world. It is set in a disappeared New York City, with the smoky scent of cigarettes hanging over all, men playing chess, the racket of the elevated subways, the feel of life lived underground, everything a little bit beat. And *Beat Generation* is pervaded by the music of conversation.

Working in spurts, Kerouac spewed this "spontaneous bop prosody", or "jazz poetry". The play (and the novels) are everything and the kitchen sink too. It is a kind of demolition-derby pile-up, a jazzy musical of words picking up speed and hurling themselves forwards – in a bumper-car version of dialogue. *Beat Generation* is about talking and friendship and shooting the shit, it is about the biggest question of all – existence. Kerouac and his rough-hewn characters – just this side of hobos – want to know how and why we exist and then in some spontaneous combustion they come to know that in the end there are no answers, there is just the moment we are in, and the people around us.

Here is the romance of the road, rebirth and karma – Kerouac's peculiar and deeply personal combination of the working man discussing astral bodies, karmic debt, past lives and the selling of Jesus. Here is the power of ideas and the difficulty of escaping belief. And here is the love of God and the fear of God – despite Kerouac's interest in the alternative, his exploration of Buddhism and eastern philosophies, he could never escape his Catholic upbringing.

Yet the play has a masculine swagger, a brand of bravado. Language and characters careen off each other in a kind of doped deliciousness, in which one feels the heat of an afternoon, the smell of hay and shit and beer at the race track, the greasy squeal of brakes, and the kind of down-and-dirty that never really washes off.

Kerouac was the man who allowed writers to enter the world of flow – different from stream-of-consciousness, his philosophy was about being in the current, open to possibility, allowing creativity to move through you, and you to be one with both process and content. It was about embracing experience rather than resisting; it is in fact the very Roman candle Kerouac writes about in *On the Road*.

On a more personal note – without Kerouac, without Jimi Hendrix, without Mark Rothko, there would be no me. I used to think Jack Kerouac was my father (sometimes literally) and Susan Sontag was my mother. I could diagram out one hell of a family tree, with Henry Miller and Eugene O'Neill as my uncles and so on. Kerouac raised me spiritually, psychologically, creatively – he gave me permission to exist.

In the end, *Beat Generation* is a treat, a sweet found under a sofa cushion. For those of us who never had enough Kerouac, now there is more.

– A.M. Homes, 2005

Beat Generation

Act One

(Scene is early morning in New York near the Bowery, standing in the kitchen, cheap kitchen, are a coloured guy called JULE *and a white guy called* BUCK, *and they're both raising glasses of wine to each other in little glasses, and* BUCK'S *saying:)*

BUCK: All right Jule, let's have one.

JULE: I wonder what the vintner buys, one half so precious as what he sells...

BUCK: Wow!... Give us another one... Hey you drink fast!

JULE: Drink! For tomorrow you may be one with yesterday's 7,000 years...

BUCK: But that's not right, you didn't get the whole thing there. Ain't you got any others?

JULE: Not now... sit, man.

BUCK: All right Jule... Here I am sitting in Julius Chauncey's kitchen in a clear cool morning in October 1955, the freshness of the day's first jug, ugh... You know Jule, there's nothing, there's no way to recreate the effect of that first glass which you get in the morning when you wake up, yet, all over the world drinkers will gobble gobble and bulp... they want more more more of what they can't have, because it can only happen once... isn't that right?... Let's have another quote, Jule.

3

JULE: No I'm tired.

BUCK: Well here we go, let's have another one… (*drinking*) I wonder where Milo is.

(*The door opens and in walks* MILO, *who is a medium-height, dark-haired fellow in a full brakeman's uniform, hat, cap, the blue uniform, the racing form in one pocket, the Bible and other books in another pocket, and a few flutes sticking out of his pocket, followed by another brakeman – but he's six foot six, fully cleanly dressed and shaved, in full conductor uniform, followed by a little tiny four-foot-eleven not-quite-midget in a full suit with vest, hatless… they are* MILO, SLIM *and* TOMMY.)

BUCK: Hey there you are, I knew you'd get here… Well well well, look at all these brakemen's uniforms here… Winos and brakemen getting together early in the morning, hey?

TOMMY: Hey there Buck, what you say, boy?… Say can I sit at the table, Vicki? (*as a girl, white girl, comes in from the other room, having heard the visitors arrive*) Can I sit at the table and dope out these horses? Today I've got a couple horses running at Jamaica – I'd give my left arm if I could go out and play them at the track but there's a little matter of a job at Riker's at two o'clock, durnit.

MILO: All right Tommy… you move over the end there Tommy m'boy, that's right, Buck sits on the floor so's me and old long tall Slim Summerville here can resume our best four-out-of-seven series championship chips

4

chess game of the world... (*looking at Vicki*) Ah, just what I like to see in the morning, boys and girls. You got any coffee Vicki?

VICKI: Yes I have some, I'll warm it up here.

MILO: Just a little bit of sugar in that coffee Vicki, m'dear.

VICKI: Yes *sir*.

MILO: Well now listen here, old buddy Buck (*taking out the chessboard and pieces*), so it's true as you do say, that God *is* us, is just us, right here, now, exactly as you say, we don't have to run to God because we're already there, yet Buck, really, now face it old buddy that sonumbitch trail to heaven is a *long* trail—

BUCK: Wal, that's just words...

MILO: Boy, we start out in our astral bodies, man, and you know the way a ghost go when headin' out there to that bright blank night go in a straight line, that, and then, as he wanders, just astral-born and new to the game he gets to wigglin' and a-goin' from side to side, that is, to explore, much as H.G. Wells says about a maid sweepin' out a hall from side to side, the way migrations advance?...

VICKI: What are you *talkin'* about again?

MILO: And so astral, he'll go migrate out there to the next or martian level where he bumps into all them *levels* you see, but with that spectral astral special interprenation... how do you pronounce that, inter-pe-ne-tration speed.

BUCK: Words.

MILO: True... true... but then after... now lay out these things Slim, I'll take the... I'll tell you what we'll do, I'll take the black, you take the white, I'm going to give you a chance today so now listen Buck, here was a guy who had such a bad aura of traitorship around him, in fact he was a later entity of Judas, he'd, or people'd sense him, sense him and turn in the street and say, "Who's that *betrayer* just went by?" – all of his life suffering from some curse people had of him, which was that karmic debt he had to pay for selling Jesus for a handful of silver—

BUCK: Words... I keep saying "words". Milo and I really mean it, I'm trying to get you to say "God is Words"... It's *still* all words, ain't it?

MILO: No no no no no no no no no no no... When that astral body gets to Saturn certain conditions there may seek... might get to change him into a rock and so on, you gotta watch out boy, you want him to turn into a rock?

BUCK: Tell me seriously Milo, doesn't the entity go to God in heaven?

MILO: That it does, after a long trail and trial, you see... hmm. (*lighting a cigarette suavely*)

6

BUCK: Ah words.

MILO: Words as you will.

BUCK: Or birds...

MILO: Till finally, purified and so spotless to be like the garment that was never rented, the entity *does* arrive in heaven and back to God, so is why I say we're not there now.

BUCK: How can we help not being there now? We can't be anywhere else... the world, or heaven, is what form is... We can't avoid our reward... heaven so sure, Milo.

MILO: Ahh... All right Slim your move, you're white.

TOMMY: Hey Milo you wanta look at the sheets I worked out?

MILO: No, I don't have to look at anything, I tell you I've got it made.

JULE: The horses?... You've got the horses made, how you got it made?

MILO: Sit down here Slim, and we'll take out these, ah... we'll take out a fielding lance at each other's hide... Pawn to king four? By God I know how to answer you, I'll lay my Bible here beside me in case I got something to quote to old Buck there sittin' on the floor, that unbeliever... Vicki you got that coffee ready yet? Just a little bit of sugar, you know, nothin' fancy, unless Buck wants to run out and buy pork chops with that w-i-n-e money he's about to run out with and buy wine.

BUCK: No no no, you look over all the form charts for the day, find only horses that have won thirty-three per cent of their races, and especially run within the last eight days dropping weight *and* running their favourite distance, several other items...

MILO: Pawn to king four, hey?... Well, we'll try knight here, we'll try knight here.

SLIM: Knight to bishop five.

BUCK: How many times Milo have I told you you can't beat the horses – my father lost his *business* doin' it, man... 'Course years later he kept sayin' that he lost his business on account of some flood or other but... it was that old mutuel flood, boy.

MILO: Yass yass yass, your move big buddy.

TOMMY: Running a mile and a sixteenth in 1:43 flat comes to a mile and an eighth today, I don't know, I don't know if he can stand another... another half a furlong.

BUCK: Bearing impost of seventeen hundred thousand million pounds he will find sumpin'...

MILO: Lazy Charley, Lazy Charley, why you, man, don't you realize they found that guy dead on the racetrack with forty thousand dollars worth of uncashed tickets in his pocket, he had 'em so figured out – now wait a minute now man, now look here – honey that's right, just a little bit of sugar, that's right, fine.

VICKI: Eggs?

MILO: Eggs, eggs... fine, fine, fine, FINE... hmm, it's better than Chinatown.

VICKI: Anybody else?

MILO: Sunny side up and a bit of hot strong coffee to go with it, you know, make some more coffee, and I like it pipin' hot.

JULE: (*singing bop*) Swap swapa diddleya deel do.

TOMMY: There oughta be a hole in there for him to sneak through, you know?

JULE: Did you find my pussy last night Tommy, huh Tommy did you find a nice little old broad lyin' on the sidewalk and take her to you know, you know, your pad?

TOMMY: Not last night Jule, I was – I just had a few beers in the Pink Angel and there was a couple of old gals there but they didn't appeal to me too much, too drunk.

JULE: Did you make it with any big old broads last night Tommy? Did you did you did you did you *did* you?

VICKI: Oh Jule!

JULE: Swing, somebody, swing!

BUCK: Yeah.

JULE: Yeah.

MILO: Well now old Lazy Charley see...

SLIM: ...all right I'll move this bishop...

MILO: ...he gets up there in the club lounge you know, and he's comin' post time, he's standin' there by the fifty-dollar window and the warning buzzer rings, Old Charley takes one casual look to see who's third choice and lays the money *down*... That's why I wanta go to the racetrack today because man I tell *you* – and don't you see really it's all really worked out for us in advance and all we gotta do is pile right on... that's why I say I wanta go to that racetrack today, I gotta win that money back, and besides – the money I lost, you know – and there's something I want you to know, how many times have I gone to that bettin' window and asked the man for number five because somebody just then said "number five" and the ticket I'd originally wanted was number two, and I'm standin' there you know, and I'm lookin' around, and instead of buyin' my number two, which goes accordin' to Lazy Charley's system, I buy number five.

BUCK: Why don't you just say, "Give me number two instead of number five, I made a mistake" – wouldn't he give it back to you? The guy that sells the tickets there?

MILO: Hmm, well... because there was a disincarnate entity telling me number five, I believe that it was trying to help...

BUCK: Sometimes you just hear them in your head?

MILO: Yeh, and it may be trying to let me win or lose with the certainty of the foreknowledge of the outcome of that race, old buddy, don't you think I don't know, why pshaw boy, I got – and you know Lazy Charley never said he was ever gonna deviate from that third choice.

BUCK: So at least you know that disembodied ghost entities are trying to make you lost because you say that the third choice can't fail!

MILO: Can't.

VICKI: What do they look like?

BUCK: What?

VICKI: The dis-arnate eninnies... the disarnate entities there.

MILO: *All* kinds of ways... auras, auras – say for instance that betrayer that I told you about there, scared everybody down down the street, auras that are showin' ogres of the imagination opers anyway and he's runnin' down the street there, everybody knew that in a previous lifetime he had been a great betrayer, and he carried that along with him as he went along—

BUCK: Yeah, big seedy ghosts amplin' down the line into that endless sky, shoot, man, Milo why, what are you talkin' about?

MILO: Now look, you just listen to me boy and I'm gonna show you somethin', hm, boy and you know that Jesus Christ, he comes down and his karma on earth is to know that he is the son of God assigned to die for the safety, the eternal safety of mankind; it's all arranged ahead of time, even Judas—

BUCK: Well, and all the lives of *ants* are arranged ahead of time?

MILO: No, not ants. Knowing it, Jesus, he does it, dies on the cross, that was his karma as Jesus, don't you understand?... Dig what that means...

BUCK: Okay.

MILO: So, ah, back to Lazy Charley... you see now that cool Charley, he didn't have to sweat and jump in the crowd, men... he collects his uncashed tickets...

BUCK: ...and dies.

MILO: Yeah that's right, and from there he goes on to whatever his karma demands of him... er, the next planet, or the next aura, wherever he has to go next he'll do it... Ain't nothin' worrying him... Came on earth to devise a system to beat the horses and left earth.

BUCK: What's this book here you got?

MILO: That's Edgar Cayce...

BUCK: That's Edgar Cayce, you know about Edgar Cayce, Jule, old Okie guy you know, come in a house with someone sick, and goes by the bed of the sick person and loosens his tie and gets down on the couch flat on his back, and there's his wife sittin' by the bed with a pad and pencil and there's this sick person there, see, and old Cayce goes into a trance; finally she says, "Edgar!" as he goes into his trance, "why does Midget Bloobloo got thrombophlebitis in this hard-ass earth, what's he done to deserve it and how is he going to cure it?"

MILO: That's right.

SLIM: What's this?

BUCK: Edgar Cayce... see, and Edgar Cayce lyin' there and says: "Edgar Dwapdwap here in a previous lifetime..."

MILO: Previous lifetime that's right... white moves.

BUCK: "...was a Aztec priest in the hills of old Teotihuacán where they shed his pumpin' heart, he shed more blood of victims and drank it by the buckets and blood and sawdust and saw fires, finally now to atone for those sins he's been reborn with an excess of blood that thickens the clots in his veins and makes it work his karma, his earned fate, his fate he earned, by suffering now, he has to pay back for that, and that's why he has this blood disease…" So that, and then…

TOMMY: Hey, there's a blood clot in this egg!

MILO: Throw it away!

TOMMY: That's a little chicken in there, I ain't gonna throw it away…

BUCK: How come that this Edgar Cayce never predicted the horses?

MILO: Because, man, that is another, and that is a different kind of information now, now he cured the guy with sickness, like you say, he discovered why he had it, and then he gave him the cure, which was whatever it was, because this information otherwise that – he *could* – have predicted the horses but didn't, or wouldn't, because it was forbidden information – you'll hear all about that tonight old buddy when you and I my day's totals are at least run off, the whole thing mathematically should be ready tomorrow, *one*, we tie up that train boy and get in my car where Irwin, you and Paul be waitin', and I suppose this Manuel's comin' to the track with us, ain't he, and Paul – and so we'll drive out to my pad out there, and the Bishop's comin' tonight to give us all a polite talk.

TOMMY: The Bishop? Bishop who?

MILO: The Bishop Hartori there…

SLIM: Ah, you mean the guy Cora goes to hear.

MILO: Yeah, you know, that... give him my... My God she gave him my only good floor lamp, can't even see in the living room any more, hmm.

BUCK: *Floor* lamp? For what?

MILO: Well, for his lecture hall.

BUCK: What Church is this guy?

MILO: Oh it's the Ref... the new, ah, Aramaean Church I believe they call it.

BUCK: And you mean we're all going to have to see this guy tonight?

MILO: In my house.

BUCK: What is he wearing?

MILO: Well, he wears long black robes, and he has a big crucifix hanging down... just a young kid, twenty-eight, real hepcat... He's gonna be there with his old aunts, you know...

BUCK: And Irwin... Paul... and all these people?

MILO: Yeah, and you, and... others. Oh, Cora moppin' up the house and gettin' ready all day and sendin' out post-cards and being all excited and lookin' for more lamps...

BUCK: Well, ah, by God, I ain't – I'm lookin' forward to the racetrack but what am I gonna do with a *bishop*?

MILO: Oh show him anything you want, and explain to him the fact – in fact he knows all about that, man, why shit that guy there ain't nothin' he don't know about... Aurobindo,* y'know.

VICKI: Jule, I haven't got enough plates.

MILO: That's all right baby, put it all in one plate and we'll split right down the middle and sideways and as many's people gonna eat and just chew off.

BUCK: And me drunk, already drunk last night with Maguire, and only just had a few hours on Jule's couch and to meet the *Bishop*? Do I have to be on my best behaviour? What am I gonna do, and the racetrack too?

TOMMY: Ah what are you complainin' about Buck, you have a pretty nice life, I never seen you sweat for much.

BUCK: I sweat for what I sweat for. Listen Milo, where's Irwin now?

MILO: He'll meet us at the car at six-fifteen when we take the racetrack train back – we tie it up, and I'm off duty.

TOMMY: Chesterfield will win the sixth race, by God I'm gonna place a bet on him.

MILO: That third choice hasn't – bishop to rook five –

that third choice for two days stopped and that is exactly seventeen races he missed now, now he's bound *dead-bang* sure to come in today, no doubt about it, and if he misses, it'll be twenty-five straight and I ain't never heard of that yet at Jamaica, or anywhere, though Lazy Charley did say in that article that they had there in *Turf* or somethin', he'll sometimes miss as much as thirty straight, and boy that's when you gotta have that *reserve* in the bank, and faith.

JULE: Ah, why do you wanta make a whole lot of money anyway, I mean everybody likes money, but that's all you *talk* about, man... Here you are working on the railroad making 650 dollars a month and you have your chick, and your pad, and your kids, and you just keep talking and talkin' about *money*.

MILO: It isn't for *money*, no sir, not at all, it's philanthropy. Now Buck here, you cover the California tracks, see, I'll... I'll wire him the money and – the New England tracks that is – and Tommy the Florida tracks, see Ole Tommy out there runnin' around pattin' the asses of all them young girls down there in Florida? We'll get old Jule here to cover the Chicago tracks near St Louis so he can be close to home there and see all his old broads there... and down in New Orleans we'll send out Irwin there, soon as I learn him to do this properly and play the system, gotta wait you know till the last minute with his eyeballs glued to that tote board, and old rubber number two's gonna have to send him. Paul there? His buddy, we're gonna have to send him to Russia to cover them Russian tracks out there, and get some Mexican cat

17

to cover Aguascalientes, boy, and pretty soon we'll send Marlon Brando to cover tracks in France or somethin', have a network of buddies, million-dollar organization – we can build up soup kitchens, monasteries, devote all that karma you see, work out our karma and go off when we die with somethin' that will enable us to go off into the future, our future life in outer space, with some new kind of... *credit*... and turn all that around, 'cause you know man there's not enough time for all the things that's got to be done, not enough *money*, only do you realize – sonumbitch that pawn has got to go! (*pfuit, sweeping off pawn*) Say kid, do you need any help with those eggs there baby? Um, hah? What's the idea of giving the eggs to Tommy first – just because he's smaller than I am don't mean that I'm not as hungry as he is, you know.

JULE: Buck, go out and get that next poor boy.

BUCK: I still need three more cents. Milo give me a nickel.

MILO: I'll give you a nickel, and tomorrow providing I'm sending you to Jamaica to contrive that line, boy, that third choice don't hit today, it's *bound* to hit tomorrow you see, we go out today together... if it misses today you've got to be out there *dead sure* tomorrow and get on that percentage!

BUCK: Okay Milo, that's sure.

MILO: Now I'm gonna give you three hundred dollars tomorrow, and thirty-eight cents for a poor-boy pint of wine that you can drink on a haystack when the races are done.

BUCK: Yeah, I'll be drinkin' on a haystack when the races are done, watchin' jockeys drivin' away in Cadillacs, and airplanes landing at Idlewild.

MILO: That's right boy, and airplanes landing at Idlewild with all that money in the sky.

BUCK: Why can't you come with me tomorrow?

MILO: Tomorrow's Saturday, that's my gig with the Montauk train, Ole 38, Montauk and back.

SLIM: I'll be on the local to Huntington.

VICKI: You want 'em soft or hard?

MILO: Anyway you like baby, I'll be hard, you be soft.

BUCK: What's happened to that model that was gonna have her picture taken by Filipino we saw last week?

TOMMY: Which one was that?

MILO: Oh I ran into that Chinee girl, I haven't seen her since.

TOMMY: What Chinee girl?

MILO: She got my Victrola,* she just got everthing, *Wee*

19

*Small Hours** and my Webcor three-speed box...* Man, I shouldna done it, aaff.

JULE: I'll make the run?

BUCK: Will you?

TOMMY: Go, man, go, I'll have a blast...

MILO: (*singing*) Fine day, fine day, I can see this is gonna be my lucky day; I have this dog-eared brakie here from El Paso Texas, six foot six and lookin' down on me from the upper heights of the cold mountains so tied up in his long suspenders – fat chances outa one that Slim you're sunk, pal.

SLIM: Guess I am.

MILO: Got you cornered, boy, got you cornered... Now you can't make a move outa there... there is one move you could do but I ain't gonna tell you what it is, natcherly, and I reckon you could figure it out in a while but I ain't gonna tell you what it is.

BUCK: Neal wins the World Series? The first game of the World Series? What about that bishop over there?

MILO: Huh? What bishop?

BUCK: Yeah, it is a checkmate.

MILO: Checkmate indeed.

JULE: That's the way the ball bounces.

MILO: (*sweeping the chesses off the board*) We're ORF!

SLIM: Now wait, wait wait a minute, wait a minute, put 'em back where you had 'em, I had an idea, I wasn't checkmate there... For one thing you can put that knight over there to show me the position, you didn't put it back but I could see it – if the knight was back there... where was it, put it back there.

MILO: Here?

SLIM: No no, on the other side... er, it was closer... it was a black check knight, the bishop was there.

MILO: The bishop was there?

SLIM: The bishop wasn't there?

BUCK: How can you tell now?

MILO: We're ORF to the races and it's Lazy Charley taking the lead (*and here* MILO *starts to put the chesses away in his pocket in the box*) at the clubhouse, turn there's your – darling, marvellous eggs just fluffy and light (*as the girl brings the eggs*), hmm just like my baby's puddin', hoo!... and now listen now old Buck, now old wild sonumbitch, don't you get drunk today on that w-i-n-e 'cause boy, we've got – who's got a cigarette, I'm fresh out – we've got to go out there, and we've got something to do *today*.

BUCK: Finish up that fifth, Jule.

JULE: Here.

BUCK: Okay, some left.

JULE: You better drink, you better drink, you better drink (*singing*)... hum... and it's oh the greatest, the greatest, the greatest...

(JULE *goes out, closes the door, he's going out to get the wine.*)

MILO: Butter, butter! Where's the butter? Ain't there no bread around here? Ain't there no Follies Girls or anything? Have to run out there in the Olympic Series and do the standing broad jump all by myself... looking for your eyes I was, in Akron, for a glimpse of your eyes...

SLIM: I'll take this piece of butter... I'll take this piece here and butter it up real careful, and eat it real slow, I'll eat this side on the plate.

MILO: Don't you invade my territory while I eat on this side, except for a little bit of yellow there, pal.

SLIM: Well you can have that yellow, but I'll take that cookie.

MILO: What cookie? Ack, ow, you dawg, snap!... Now boys we're short on time... (*looks at his watch*) How's your old timepiece there Slim... short on time. (*They both look at their watches.*) Your timepiece there's all right?

SLIM: I see forty-two.

MILO: I got forty-one and one half... dammit... forty-one and three quarters... who's right and who's wrong?... Coffee, ah coffee, slurp, good old hot holy way-I-like-it telling you, Tommy, coffee; you just washin' your river underwear when you're tryin' to figure out them horses; you're wastin' your time, boy; I'm tellin' you about Lazy Charley, he's *right*.

TOMMY: Listen man, I've been playin' the horses since before you were born, remember that, I'm much older than you are.

BUCK: Did you ever hear that story about the time Tommy and Denis played the horses, Milo? Tommy had to deliver a Buddha statue to Riverside Drive in some kind of seabag and wanted to make the daily double and so he rushed, after he delivered he rushed to the racetrack on time, and there's Denis up in the clubhouse with some fancy dolls and they see this little guy rushing through the crowd with this big empty bag on his back, and the girl turns to him and she says, "What's Tommy doing with that *huge* bag?" and Denis says, "Tommy's got the horses figured out so well today he thought he'd bring a big bag."

MILO: Mdah.

BUCK: And the girl believed it.

23

SLIM: A big bag to put all his money in, huh?

BUCK: And the girl believed it.

TOMMY: Wasn't exactly like *that*.

MILO: More butter? Okay then it's mine... hup whoop, now wait a second here, what the hell do you mean about time? Now it's forty-three isn't it... for krissakes all I hear is talk about time and God around here... Yass sir... Haven't had so much in there, nice front, nice side, nice hippies, flippy dippy.

TOMMY: Who's that?

MILO: Well I'm lookin' at a picture in the paper here, flippy dippy, that's the way I figure it myself; shooting star of mercy shoulda had a bleak face, heh?

BUCK: There's another one, oh is she a gone cutie though ain't she? (*looking over* MILO'S *shoulder at the paper*)

MILO: Where where?

BUCK: She's gone.

MILO: Oh *man*, let's eat... let's eat... and now, (*stretching*) ah now... children... this foolishness is... short on time, it's forty-three and a half now men, we're ready to go?

BUCK: What about Jule?

MILO: Well he's not coming to the racetrack, now I've got exactly twenty-eight minutes to make that on duty, and there's a sweet little baby pussy I want you to see on the way, goin' to give us exactly or maybe less than that, *clean*, about – ooh I don't know – about, if she's in, we'll have maybe we'll have one minute... (*drops ashtray on the floor, picks it up*) Er, but boys, stayin' around in Jule Chauncey's kitchen here, we're being *ostracized* here, we gotta get on down the line there... Yes sir, we're ready to roll? Hm, and, hey look at this one here, that's some nice little sweet sumpin', do you hear that – dig that little dress? Now all on account of this *Manuel* ideas of yours, Buck, the cat you want us to go to the racetrack of yours, Buck, the cat you want us to go to the racetrack with, now we're gonna be late for the racetrack and we gotta...

BUCK: Manuel's a great guy.

MILO: I mean... we can't see the little girl if we have to go get *him*.

BUCK: I promise you, I know.

MILO: Well, *man*.

BUCK: Why don't you like him?

MILO: He's one of those guys, you know, don't do you no good.

BUCK: Why? They got 'em rough and mean, but Manuel's a great poet, a great kid.

MILO: Wiggle though that as you will but I don't understand him.

BUCK: Why, because he keeps yelling in a loud voice? That's the way he talks.

MILO: Not that... just, man don't you know me, I know, I've known him... but...

BUCK: Ah he's a good kid, he's no – he's our *friend*.

MILO: The friend's so-si-e-tay.

BUCK: All right.

MILO: I see here that we now have... where did all those guys go?... Eh, you can sit here and I'll sit over here, then we'll go down we'll go see my baby pussy and we're gonna go get M-a-n-u-e-l to go to the racetrack with us and we have just enough time Tommy to have a little – but now wait a minute now... we do have three minutes, two and a half at the most, now what we've got to have is another piccolo for Buck – now wait a minute.

TOMMY: I got one here.

MILO: Well you've got one, now here's – we're gonna have a trio, did I ever tell you that one about the – there once was a man from Canute, (*they take out their flutes*) had warts on his cheroot, he poured acid on these, and now when he pees, he fingers his cheroot like a flute? D'I ever tell you that? (*everybody laughing and high*) Never heard that one? We gotta, also we can hear the trio, and we'll trade off... Now you'll play the white piccolo, Buck you play the black piccolo, I'll play the sweet potato* for one minute and then you'll take the sweet potato, we'll pass it around in rotation, see, so we don't get on any bum kicks because of the poor instrument. *Sit down!* Sit down to the quartet, the Beethov... come on, string quartet man – this is a clarinet trio, you unnerstand. (*experimental flutings*)

TOMMY: Who's gonna pass on his ability here?

MILO: On ability Vicki herself will pass on.

TOMMY: Is she listening?

MILO: No, we don't, no we just want a three-way here...

TOMMY: A little cooperation here.

(SLIM *drums on inverted saucepan.*)

MILO: Listen, for real tea-head goof kicks, man, you can't have any – we gotta be like a string quartet, no beat and syncopation whatsoever, see, and we'll just goof you unnerstand, like a string quartet, you unnerstand, but he'll play his solo there, you know like he just did, drum solo, see... Let's make sure we're getting everything here. (*adjusts chair to face* VICKI... *first notes, challenges of flutes*) Hey, man, the guy who has the soft one must be sure and get his thing to hear close enough so Vicki can hear.

TOMMY: I can't hear my thing...

MILO: No yours can be heard, yours is the loudest, you sit like this, and Buck's about right, he might turn that way a little, but I have to keep turning that way... Now let's goof again, let's goof again, (*laughing, tittering maniacally*) I didn't mean to interrupt and all this 'cause you guys...

BUCK: Well as you say it all goes down the same hole.

TOMMY: Hey I got to get a girl to give me incentive.

MILO: (*fluting*) That was, ah, that was amazing, I began to think of snake charmers and then I began to think of the, toot toot toot, and so therefore I had to cut you all a great mighty solo, my mighty solo was about to come in there.

TOMMY: Oh, the rape charmers!

MILO: Ready? (*announcing*) The rape charmers of the Indian Plantation System... (*All three play, as* SLIM *listens in the saucepan.*)

Clarity of tone!

TOMMY: Ah!

MILO: An attribute.

TOMMY: Yes Sahib. (*They play.*)

MILO: Slowly, children, slowly. (*They play slowly.*) Now we trade! Now we trade! (*grabbing* TOMMY'S *piccolo*)

TOMMY: Hey!

MILO: We gotta get accustomed to all the instruments.

TOMMY: Hey geez hey.

MILO: No, like we – hee hee – come on go on, music, there you are. (*handing sweet potato to* TOMMY)

TOMMY: What is the hole here?

MILO: That's it, see.

TOMMY: Hey what's this little tiny hole here? This isn't a... what kinda hole is that hey!

MILO: Never seen a hole that small before.

TOMMY: Is this the small hole?

MILO: It's the small hole, the mighty seven holes and the mighty seven epistles. (TOMMY *blows.*) All wind... all hollow blowing... The hole's up here... There you are.

SLIM: Hey Milo, short on time!

MILO: Hup hup. (*picks up chessboard, chessmen, Bible, racing form*) Here we go men!

BUCK: So long Vicki, so long, see you later. Short on time.

VICKI: What?

BUCK: Short on time!

(*And they rush out. And after about ten seconds the girl sits in the chair and puts her head in her hands and laughs... and then the door opens and* JULE, *her husband, walks in.*)

VICKI: (*looking up*) Milo was short on time.

JULE: Short on *time*!... You know what Buck said...

VICKI: ...you want to?

JULE: ...kiss her *belly*! Sure, I'll see what I can do about giving you a smack of H today... And now I'm gonna have a glass of wine... How many sands are there to be removed from the Pacific Ocean, each time you pour a million gallons of joy juice into the emptiness of all space, and does it even matter? (*drinks*)

Act Two

Scene One

(*First race... arm in arm,* MILO *in the middle, wearing full brakeman's uniforms got both arms around* BUCK *and the new cat* MANUEL, *and* MANUEL'S *saying:*)

MANUEL: Yay you guys, wow, you told me you'd get me at twelve o'clock sharp and you were half an hour late...

MILO: Midnight.

MANUEL: *Mid*-night? You told me, damn you, that you was gonna be... yah I know you, I know it's all plots, everywhere it's plots, everybody wants to hit me over the head and deliver my body to the tomb!... The last time I had a dream about truth it was you, it was you, it was you two, and it was much more with golden birds, though, and all sweet fawns consoled me, I was the consoler, I lifted my skirts of divinity to all the little children who trudged by, I changed into Pan, I piped them sweet green tune, right under a tree, and you were that tree... Milo you were that tree! I see it all now, you can't follow me!

MILO: Well, ah, that's perfectly all right my boy, it's that breach of time when you see a pedestrian or a car or an upcoming crack-up just crack right on up, nothin's going to happen, if it don't separate you got that extry breach of time to sure give 'em grace but ordinarily ten times outa one boy them astral bodies separate cat and

31

that's because it's all figured out in the hall up there where they make the cee-ga-ree-los!

MANUEL: Ach! Milo I can't stand you, you, you give me nothing but bull, he pulls my ears, it'll never end, I quit, I give up – what time is the first race, man? here we are!

BUCK: Manuel's a razzer! Manuel the Razzer! One of them guys likes to razz the boys, you know.

MILO: The time of the first race is about out of reach now, thanks to all these various developments... Naturally we can't play the daily double.

BUCK: Who wants to play the daily double anyway? The odds are never long enough, it's a hundred-to-one, a fifty-to-one chance you got pickin' two successive winners and all they give you is, like, seven-to-one and all that.

MANUEL: Daily double?

MILO: Yes, sir, daily double... but speakin' about – now – let's get back here now, that horse, now I'll tell you now, that this – ah, and so, I was telling you, the third choice horse paid six dollars to show yesterday, three to five dollars, and he paid five dollars to show twice, and then four three times, a little under four, about twenty, forty cents, *twice*, came in the money all day first second and third *all day*, now you realize what that means?

MANUEL: Numbers! Numbers!

MILO: Now... let's... you... here we are at the racetrack now, let's not... now what we should do and inasmuch as you don't believe me both of you, I beg you to see and to understand – I'll tell you what I'll – I'll play win all day, according to Lazy Charley's system, third choice – now Lazy Charley, now you realize Manuel he was an old hand at bettin' that system and when he died they found him dead at the racetrack right in that clubhouse there, forty thousand dollars worth of uncashed tickets in his chest, which means that by that time he was plankin' real heavy and affectin' the odds himself, why God just yanked him right out of this earth because he was gonna upset it.

MANUEL: But I've only got three dollars!

MILO: This'll come in time... (*and he removes his arms from around the two fellows*) Boy when I get really rollin' I'm gonna start building monasteries and Samsarean retreats and hand out five-dollar bills to deserving bums in skid row and in fact even people in trolleys then I get me a Mercedes Benz boy and just go spinning down to Mexico City on that El Paso Highway doing 165 on the straightaways and boy you *know* that's gotta be in low gear 'cause when you come to that curve you gotta make it at eighty or a hundred and it's gotta swash that car through, it's a matter of side-swiping that curve with your *brakes*, yes *sir*! Now what we'll do, I'll play to win, Manuel play to place, Buck play to show, all day on the third choice.

BUCK: I haven't got no money, I've got thirty-five cents...

I ain't gonna *bet*, I ain't got no money... Let's get a beer, somebody buy me a beer... It's beer and baseball and hotdogs.

MILO: Now just a minute here boy, now third choice in the betting means I'm gonna bet on, ah—

MANUEL: I'm gonna bet on number nine! It's a mystical number! It's Dante's mystical number!

MILO: *Nine? Nine?* Why that dog's goin' off at thirty-to-one... Now look here, old buddy, see here we are at the racetrack, and there's your flags flyin' on the flagpoles and here she is the bugle call, now we're alone now and we're all set and I've got a chance to really talk to you fellas and tell you a few things, I want you to *know* how to win at the races.

BUCK: How's your horse running, your third choice in the second race?

MILO: Where? What? Right now she's number six, you see, 'course all that can change as the bottom of the hat.

BUCK: What was that you wanted to tell me about when we got out of the train?

MILO: I'm feelin' so fine, Buck, Manuel, I'm feelin' *so* good on this great afternoon... here we are and we're gonna make some money and talk – can't you hide that bottle better there boy – we're gonna—

BUCK: It's only a poor-boy, it's almost finished... here, there, I'll finish it and throw it in the wastebasket.

MILO: That's right, I'm gonna buy you a beer...

BUCK: We'll be respectable drinkin' outa cartons, won't we?

MILO: That's right, ole daddy, and now *tonight*, this is after we do all this bettin' and winnin' here—

BUCK: Hey look, look at the tote board, he's changed to seven!

MILO: That's right, seven it is, seven times seven is forty nine times my brother's been hurt, we'll just stand here by the window real close and sneak in that line when the warning buzzer rings, now Mannie you come along.

BUCK: How much have you lost in the last two days?

MILO: Last two days, man I'm five thousand in the hole now.

BUCK: Five *thousand*! Is that all that money you got for breaking your rib? What's... the wife sayin'?

MILO: Aw naturally she doesn't know about it and I don't want you to tell her about it, I got my baby pudding in mah pocket right here, I got joy in my back pocket.

BUCK: All right, let me see it.

MILO: She's in, it's over there, it's over there, it's over there.

BUCK: Look, Milo, there's a new flash, you know I hope it stays seven because you know that kid is a good rider, Valenzuala, that little Mexican cat boy he really can drive a horse, dammit, what strong wrists those little guys have… you know when I was a kid I used to go to the racetrack with my father and my—

MILO: That's all right my boy, now listen now, we're gonna wait at the beer counter here and as the betters merge into long panicky lines waiting as the horses near the six furlong pole and the buzzer's gonna go, you know, and they all hustle and push and line up and so on, we just wait till the last minute cool and collected like old Lazy Charley, nobody's even once gonna look out at the actual horses but we're gonna know all about the numbers, you see, them astral numbers… Now you can have the cigar smoke and shuffling feet, yah.

BUCK: Hey look over here, over that crowd, over that field, and that distant Jamaica gas tank across the roofs far away, it's Jamaica Racetrack Long Island New York but it's definitely an ant heap in nirvana, ain't it… Those cars out there on that little highway are smaller than I can believe, it's a… space trick! And look at those jockeys!

MILO: All right boys, now we're gonna line up here, as soon as we finish this beer… But I'm worried about that dog 6, in spite of Lazy Charley's system – Matchstick, you know, beat Burning Bush here last Tuesday, I don't like it…

BUCK: How do you know you don't like it?

MILO: Ah, well I was looking at Tommy's form here.

BUCK: What do you have to worry about, just bet on third choice, Lazy Charley's system, that's all.

MILO: Well that's what I'm trying to tell you...

(*Meanwhile* MILO *is looking very neat and clean, it's the first race, and everybody is very cleanly dressed and there's no litter on the floor of the stage, everybody looks very happy, they're all lined up, everybody's talking.*)

Now Buck damn you I'm trying to tell you, to stick to the third choice? Sure! I wouldn't be five thousand in the hole if I had, that's why I wanted you to come with me today Buck and make me stick to the line.

BUCK: All right, Milo, I'll see to it that you stick to your system.

MILO: That's right, Buck now you get it that way, that's the whole point and the reason why I'm bringing you is that you've got to make me stick to it.

BUCK: That's right, I know what the matter with you—

MILO: That's right, I'm worried about that dog 10, that's Candle Heart boy, he can go a mile in one thirty-six, he's been running in high company around here lately too.

BUCK: Yeah but that's all right, but that's not your system.

MILO: Exactly m'boy, m'friend, exactly, we just go ahead and forget all about him don't we.

BUCK: That's right.

MANUEL: I'm gonna bet on number nine! I have a feeling and a vision about number nine! It's Dante's mystical number!

MILO: Now that's what I need is a little sense here, makes me stick to my system...... I don't know why we brought this here *Manuel*. (*aside to* BUCK)

BUCK: That's right, my boy.

(*And* MILO *puts his arm around both of them, having finished his beer, and says*:)

MILO: Now the whole point of the whole thing is I've got to get that five thousand dollars back so I can have some operation capital here you see 'cause I raise the ante up to fifty or a hundred a race and pretty soon boy I'll be plankin' in my imaginary hotter-than-Charley-prophecy that's when it'd start really makin' the money... Hey how's the back of my coat? Here's the brush, you mind brushing it off, for specks, any specks on the back of my coat?

BUCK: Few.

MILO: Brush it. (BUCK *brushes*.) That's fine good buddy, now let's see, here's a cigarette here to keep our hands contained – any specks on my shoes? How's that old handkerchief of yours? Come on down there and get down on your knees and brush them old black railroad shoes boy, I gotta look clean here, now it's clear as day, I see from the tote board here seven's gonna run off at third choice, that's our horse, right?

BUCK: Naturally.

MANUEL: I'm gonna play nine!

MILO: Manuel, what you should do is play the horse that I play all day in every one of the next seven races, but play it to place, because you see 6 is a mad dog and 10 can fly man, I've seen that dumb jockey there that's gonna ride him today fall off of him two weeks ago and he took off and came home alone by ten lengths that horse without a rider... you see, but I have dreams too, you know, Manuel, speaking of your mystical numbers.

MANUEL: Dreams?

MILO: Yeah just as a little side issue today and before we go and plank our bets now and since they're gonna be ringing the buzzer soon I'll tell you, and since I just got paid yesterday you see man now listen I had a dream that this gone little jockey cat Pulido, you know Pulido that guy you dug down in the paddock there Buck that while back, why, he—

39

BUCK: You mean the jockey that's gonna ride number nine, Manuel's horse, he was nice to the owner's little son, I remember him the other day, a real nice Mexican kid, sits on the horse digging the audience as he rides by the stands.

MILO: Yeah he's on a... Oh, in my dream in an old engine going around the track but going the wrong way, see, way out in front and in my dream the race is going from the clubhouse turn up here to the head of the stretch goin' backwards and what happens but – bam, just as they hit the win-wire going the wrong way he's ahead and the whole gol-dang train blows up, that's right men, explodes and Pulido is over the wire all by himself!

BUCK: *Man*, he really won that race!

MILO: Exactly, exactly, what's what I'm trying to tell you, and seeing all how I got my pay yesterday, I thought just for the hell of it today I'd plant a little bit side bet on Pulido in every race.

BUCK: But that's not sticking to your Charley system.

MILO: Since... that... dream... evidently... presupposes... don't you think, Manuel, that he might run three, four, maybe five mounts or even two, bring 'em in straight at any kind of price? And he's riding... he's riding... he's riding *nine*! That's Manuel's horse and dig the name, man, the name of the horse: *The Driver*! See that's the dream.

BUCK: But that's not following your system!

MILO: But as I say it was an extryspecial day, now you've got to admit yourself, Buck—

BUCK: Now wait a minute... If you don't follow your system, what are you gonna do? How long have you been losing five thousand dollars?

MILO: No, nothing, ah, nothing, ah – this is just the first dream I had, 'course baby you see I have dreams all the time, I loses money, and nobody has any money, dass iss the way it goes...

BUCK: Yeah.

MILO: And disincarnate entities, I go to the betting window, like I told you I got my third choice, say it's number one, I go up and just as I'm about to say "ten dollars to win on number one" I hear a voice say *number ten*! I come out there with a ticket on number ten!

BUCK: Yah yah yah yah yah yah yah yah.

MILO: Spirits of course, hopin' around waitin' to possess a human body soon as possible so's to get that invaluable opportunity as you know and you told me yourself about how slim the chances are of being reborn a human being, that gone turtle that swims out into infinite seas throughout eternity and comes up once in a while and sticks his head up—

BUCK: Yeah, the floating noose—

MILO: —floating noose as Buddha say, what are the chances of that turtle coming up just when the noose is over his head? Trillion to one? What long odds! You see this is our chance of being reborn a human being so as to work out the previous chance, maybe we have to lose and suffer a little bit in this world so I'm gonna play a little side bet on that dream jockey and I'm gonna play my third choice which apparently's gonna be number six now so I'm gonna go over the window now... And the air is filled with discs, ain't it, look at the discs and flying saucers up there.

MANUEL: Where?

BUCK: This very racetrack which I can see from looking at it now far across the infield, see the little cars going down the old shore – ant heap in heaven.

MILO: And so ants, and friends, how do I know that there isn't some friendly entity wants to tell me the winner... man when I hear those voices I just don't care, I mean I really hear those voices and I got to pay attention to them.

BUCK: Supposing that they were *evil* entities trying to make you lose since you're so certain that the third choice system was revealed to you to redact your karma, see, bring it back!

MILO: Man I'm telling you, I don't – listen, now. (*The*

warning buzzer rings.) There she is now, look, seven is third choice now, switched the last minute – just as clear cut third choice's I've ever seen – dammit have you got an old handkerchief I can?... Wait a minute, all right—

BUCK: Look here's a programme! (*picking one up on the ground*)

MILO: Good, no sense wasting a quarter on them damn things.

BUCK: Buy me another beer when they're off huh as soon as you've placed the bet.

MILO: Man I have exactly twenty-one ten-dollar bills, that's for eight races—

BUCK: Well all right.

MILO: —seven... I don't wanta change – I don't wanta get hung-up on change and be short sixty cents and not be able to play that full potential percentage man in the eighth race, it's got to come.

BUCK: Manuel can you buy me a beer?

MANUEL: Sure, man.

MILO: You wait right here, fellas.

MANUEL: I'm goin' with you!

MILO: That's all right I'll be right back.

(*So* MANUEL *and* MILO *go to the placing window and they place their bets and come back together.*)

BUCK: Who'd you bet?

MILO: Third choice of course.

BUCK: But you've got three tickets there, let me see.

MILO: *Four.*

BUCK: *Four* tickets?

MILO: Well you see I figured out that this dream jockey and then my third choice Lazy Charley, and I was worried about that dog 10 and that other dog 6...

BUCK: Put no stock in dreams and omens, oh *man!*...

MILO: I just put a little side bet on that dog that Tommy was talking about, I knew he was going to cause trouble.

BUCK: All right, all right... how can you follow Lazy Charley's system, you won't make any profit this way if you're going to make any at all.

MILO: That's the way it's been all along, man.

BUCK: Well that's how you've been losing five thousand dollars, why don't you control yourself!

MILO: (*whispering*) That's what I was trying – the next race – oh look at Manuel there, he's just coming back with his ticket there, number nine.

BUCK: But Milo you brought me here to make you stick to your system!

MILO: That's right old buddy and you've been doing very well!

BUCK: I ain't been doing so good, you're sort of – why are you so resigned about your own madness!

MILO: Every night I pray that I'll stick to that third choice, I'll tell you that much.

BUCK: Well by God, I don't know…

(*And the race is run: "They're off!" "And it's Burning Bush taking the lead, and" – all that stuff, and you know the way a race…*)

MILO: There I told ya!

(*and it's Noodles second by a length, and all the various horses*)

Pulido! Pulido! My dream jockey'll do it!

(*"Half-mile pole, it's the half-mile pole" and so on so the race is run and you get all that stuff on the stage, and so:*)

45

BUCK: Well Milo, that horse of yours they'll be bringin' him by lamplight in my dreams.

MILO: Good! When third choice comes in third naturally that's as it should be, right? Seein' as how he was third choice he should third-choice it to the public's satisfaction, good God man just let him lose *all* he wants, the more he loses the stronger I get, because the percentage is on my side after *that*.

BUCK: And what about your number nine, Manuel?

MANUEL: (*in astonishment*) How's that?

MILO: Listen, as the third choice repeatedly uses my bets increase, so that when he does come in I gain by the large bit *back* all I lost, and gain *more*.

BUCK: It's all in the numbers.

MANUEL: It's amazing, some mysteries number should come to me again, probably nine again, it's like roulette, the gambler, you know Dolgoruky* kept putting all he had on one thing, and broke the house, and I shall be like Dolgoruky, I don't care... You see Milo, Buck, if I lose it's because I'm a bum, and if I'm a – it's because I'm crap, and if I'm crap it's because the moon shines on crap! Shine on crap! Eat my babies!... Because you know every day a poem creeps up into my mind and it becomes a high poem, that's just the way I say it...

MILO: All right, all right, poetry, poetry, pickles in a barrel, boys we gotta make some money here today now... This ain't getting us nowhere here... *that* dog...

(*At this moment an old woman comes up to the three men in the play, she has big blank blue eyes and spinsterish in fact tight-bunned pioneer hair, she looks like a Grant Wood portrait, you expect to see gothic barns in back of her, sincere as all get-out... says to* MILO:)

WOMAN: Hey there Milo, bet on three and if you give me half, I have no money, huh? Just bet two dollars and if you win give me half—

MILO: You mean three in the third race? That dog, he won't win.

MANUEL: What is he? What is she? All these *mad* people around here!

MILO: Ah man, (*laughing as she goes away*) I've known her for a long time... I used to borrow money from *her*... See I bring all these people here on this racetrack train and I have to have certain relations with them, and, ah, I did get a few bets outa her one time and that little crippled newsboy there... See after the eighth race we gotta run like hell outa here and get back on that train so I can give the sign to the engineer and we go back to New York – now this here third race here, you see of course seventh choice often comes in twice a day and, ah—

MANUEL: (*looking around*) What are all these *mad* people?

MILO: You see, Manuel, if you want to win some money today you better follow *me*, now, never mind your mystical numbers, now the obvious horse in this third race clear and clean-cut a third choice as I've ever seen all alone in there at six-to-one, is old number ten!...

MANUEL: Number *two*! *That's* my favourite number!

MILO: Number two, not only is he a dog but that jockey that's ridin' him keeps fallin *off*!

BUCK: Yeah... I myself keep scanning this programme which I finally appropriated off the ground for strange hints like this horse here Classic Face sired by Manuel Champion and his dam is Erwina, or I look for stranger hints like Grandpa Buck! Or The Dreamer!... Here's one, that's weird, Night Clink, heh heh, which must mean the time I was in the clink or sumpin'... You could think of a million bets you could make... The way we're going now we'll just end up just sittin' in benches in the upper grandstand and won't be able to see the starting gate, you know it's right down there, I wanta go on the fence man. Let's go down the fence so I can explain to Manuel about how the horses – the starter in his box, how he presses the button that rings the bell, bats open the bat cages and out they lunge, man, watch those jockeys, every one of them has got a hand of steel battin' away on the horses... Like Johnny Longden, he's older than the three of us put together! Ah, and things like that you're missing.

MANUEL: Number two is my favourite number! Or either that or I'll go back to number nine.

MILO: Folly the system, man! I'm pleading with you! I told you about Lazy Charley, how they found him dead with forty-five thousand dollars worth of uncashed win tickets—

BUCK: Listen Manuel, Lazy Charley just sat around you know sippin' coffee between races, and wearing a pince-nez probably, and came out at last minute odds and saw the score and went out and made his bet and maybe went to the head a little bit, it's all in the numbers, the third choice, the consensus of the multitude reduced to a third degree which has been mathematically figured to come in as many per cent times so it just keeps givin' you bits accordin' to the losses you've suffered, you're bound to win, or bored, unless a tragic streak of lustres, or losses—

MILO: That's right, tragic! Now listen to Buck, Manuel, and you'll make some money!

MANUEL: Okay, okay, but I wanta play number two too in this race because it's my lucky number... Look at those horses, they have such skinny legs, they can get hurt. Hah? They can get hurt...

BUCK: Yeah...

Scene Two

(*Now it's the eighth race, everybody's dishevelled,* MILO'S *removed his blue brakeman's hat, blue coat, just in shirtsleeves, sleeves rolled up, undone collar, no necktie,* MANUEL'S *dishevelled, everybody's dishevelled, they're standing there:*)

BUCK: Yeah... See?

MILO: Now meanwhile—

BUCK: So what were you talking about, back there, when we got out of the train again?

MILO: Give me a cigarette, I'm all out... Wal, I was just sayin', it used to not feel couple years ago that it was hardly worth it to complete the sentence and it got so try as I might I couldn't, that's what I'm sayin', but I'm tryin' to tell you now, see, Edgar Cayce did get all his powers from one tremendous ordeal in a previous lifetime when he was a Roman soldier, and was left mortally wounded with a big spear in his back, man, on a plain, nobody to help him, took three days for him to die and during those three days he learnt how to withstand pain and content his mind and face the patient death; see it's like the Bishop says that we're gonna see tonight, the million words that he uses, long-suffering patience... Oh, we had, now, together with them other words that he uses, like sincerity of heart, and so as you think for instance and but... Hey, here comes sumpin'...

(*A blonde passes.*)

BUCK: Yeah – how long do these rebirths go on? When are you gonna lend me that book?

MILO: Just as long as there's somethin' like that walking around...

BUCK: Why doesn't God just don't step in and stop the world with a snap of his finger?

MILO: We'll just amble on over there and stand next to her, huh? Man let's go, Manuel come on, you're the one with the words, she's got a friend I see... see the brunette friend? Dig those little tight-fittin' skirts man, and besides now, come on now to get back! Now you've been saying all day long boy that we're in heaven now haven't you Buck boy?

BUCK: Yessir that's what I said, that's what I saw.

MILO: Lemme see that programme!

BUCK: (*standing hunched, hands in pockets*) Well, last race comin' up, sun goin' down.

MILO: Now, two minutes till post time, looks like number seven at this moment.

BUCK: The Cossack isn't it, a good jockey, Longden. You know why I like Longden? He won a stake race one time and I was down by the judges' stand and I didn't know who won the race, what jockey, they were all covered with mud that time. There's nothin' there but a gang of women who were there with a big silver cup to receive the winner, and I saw old John Longden suddenly standing *shorter* than all the other jockeys in the winner's circle, fifty years old riding against twenty-year-old kids, man I cried, I remember Johnny Longden trottin' across the road in Rockingham twenty-five years ago, with Jimmy Stout, who's dead now. See, the soul of Jimmy Stout's gone... Where has it gone Milo?

MILO: Out there, man, and if he didn't have fulfilled his karma you know damn well he's trottin' right up there tryin' to get back right here in this racetrack to atone for his sins in the name of Jesus Christ boy.

MANUEL: Wow you guys, why don't you concentrate on the betting! Here we've been taking trips to the men's room and the beer counter and the coffee counter and hotdogs and finally when the last race is coming up here we are, these characters of the track that looked so confident in the first race, look at them now, man! They're all looking for money in the ground, they ain't gonna find it there! Just like the thrashing doves in Chinatown, there's no hope, they have their necks cut! I don't wanta live in a world like this! And there he is, now, running around and they're looking for *women* and they're going to take them home or something, *man*... We oughta take separate leaks. Let's go back to the sweet city! I keep getting the feeling that as Milo wins he really loses and as he loses he really wins, it's all ephemeral, it can't be grabbed by the hand, it's *hurt*! The *money* can be grabbed by the hand, I wanted to buy myself a new typewriter with the money I put in but look! There's no patience in eternity! Eternity – meaning more than all time and beyond all that little crap and for ever! Milo you can't win, you can't lose, all is ephemeral, all is hurt! These are my feelings! I'm a sly gambler... but I won't gamble on *heaven*! That's the exact amount of teaching Christ gave me! Or Buddha! Or Mohammed! Or the Torah! Even if he ends up with a highly successful day, every horse comes in the money and you win you'll turn around and you say, "Buck you sonumbitch if you'd a squeezed two little measly dollars out of those jeans each race and done what I said you'd have a nice fifty-dollar bill tonight." What would Buck with a fifty-dollar bill, all he wants is thirty-five cents! But it's one of your happy days, I can see that. I can see you folding your money all proud in neat little arrangements with the small bills on the outside in your pocket. We'll come walking out of this racetrack and pass the parking lot where your little car is parked by a railroad track and I'll say, "There's your parking place, you just park there every day," and you know what you'll say to me Milo? You'll say, "Yes me boy and besides there'll be a Mercedes Benz in the place of that thing there in a few years." It's a big lake a dreams!...

MILO: Let's place the bets, it's the Angel Gabriel just made a speech and Archangel Michael is standing behind us, see how tall he is?

BUCK: Yeh, man. How's she looking now?

MILO: Who, the archangel? Er, still one... Changed from seven to one, the favourite is even money, second choice is five-to-two and he's all by himself at six-to-one... How much you s'posed to put on him now, did you figure that out on the pencil there?

BUCK: According to Lazy Charley it's forty-five dollars but I've got this figured that you've got to save a little bit of that for your dream jockey, the dead man, and that worrisome old troublesome other horse you were talking about, (*laughs*) starting to play the horses wrong with *you* now... Get me another beer will ya?

MILO: Wait here, I'll get you a beer.

BUCK: Don't *bet* too much, I'll go in line with ya.

MILO: That's all right, now Buck, that's all right, 'cause tonight we're gonna go to Huntington, we're gonna go to my pad, hear the Bishop speak, drive home in two cars, his and mine, he's bringing his two aunts you know, as I told you—

BUCK: Yeh.

MILO: And, ah, man, wait'll you see him, young cat only twenty-eight like I said a big long black – why he speaks with his eyes *closed*, you know, every now and then he looks a little bit at the congregation sittin' there in those benches and they're all quiet, you can hear their bellies rumble, sometimes he trembles, lets loose long big

Indian songs, sermons and – why shit, the wife knows all that, she sends – he sends her pamphlets and all that stuff... and...

BUCK: Manuel, what about *your* pamphlet?

MANUEL: I have a leaf in my pamphlet.

MILO: That cat.

BUCK: (*laughs*) Always bettin' on number nine because it's Dante's mystical number, say, he even says if he wins he'll buy himself a typewriter so he can write more poems.

MILO: Yeah... what about, what about if I put twenty on him?

BUCK: No! Follow your system! Supposed to put forty-five, or at least forty and five on your bloody pollution there whatever that *dream* jockey...

MILO: Well figure it on forty dollars, one to sit, five on number four to win—

BUCK: Now this is one in-carnate entity that's giving you *this* advice, I'm not *dis*-incarnate...

MILO: All right baby all right.

BUCK: And if he loses at least you'll have played your system when you come back tomorrow—

MILO: You'll come back and play it for me—

BUCK: Okay buddy.

MILO: —and the only thing for us to do now is sit and wait and man as soon as that race is over we've got to hustle back to that train because boy that *crowd*, I'm on duty you know as soon as all that.

BUCK: Where's the hog-head* and fireman that brought the train in, eating lunch in the engine or what?

MILO: No man, (*laughing*) they've been playing the horses, haven't you seen them, they're wearing business clothes you know. I come out here in my uniform but they change, you know they don't want people to know that they're playing the horses.

BUCK: You mean the whole railroad is going mad?

MILO: Well every day, you know, they put 'em on this train and they come out and they play money...

BUCK: How much do they win a day, sixty-five cents?

MILO: Well, some crippled boys make less... I'll go get your beers. (*exits*)

MANUEL: Solid! We'll make it together, Buck, you and me, we'll make it! We'll make it with Milo, we'll make a lot of money and make it on! Even though we haven't won today yet I *feel* that we'll win in this eighth race but I *see* you now, I *know* you now, Buck, you're sincere, you really want to win!

BUCK: *I don't* wanta win, *Milo* wants to win.

MANUEL: Milo!... I *believe* Milo!... I *know* he's Jesus Christ's contemporary frightening brother. I just want to – I just don't want to be hung-up on the wrong *bets*, it's like being hung-up on the wrong poets, the wrong people, the wrong *side*...

BUCK: Everything's right side Manuel actually...

MANUEL: But maybe I don't *wanta* crash, I don't wanta go to no F-f-f-f-french angel, man... *You*, Buck, I see your ideas goin' down skid row drunk with the bums, *ach*! I never even thought of doing such a thing, why bring misery on yourself? Let the dog lie. I wanta make money, I don't wanta say, "Oh ah ah I've lost my way, oh ah ah ah I've lost honey, I've lost my way," I haven't lost my way yet, I'm a young kid, I'm going to ask the archangel to let me win... Hark! I'll tell the archangel, the bright herald hears me, I hear his trumpet... (*as* MILO *returns with the beers*) Hey Milo it's ta ra tara tara tara tara, the bright herald archangel the cat with the long trombone at the start of the race, you dig that?

MILO: Yeah, yes, yes *sir*! Yes sir... There's our boy now, (*looking out*) see him out there? That Mexican kid there in the red and white silks? Goin' down the clubhouse turn? Look at the backs of those horses... *beautiful* horses! Yes sir... Mogen David wine, Mogen David wine...

BUCK: There's your horse down there!

MILO: Yes *sir*, there he is down there, at the half-mile pole he'll be still ahead by a length and a half and when Wigmo makes his move in second place and Prussia'll be third by a neck, Indian Tale'll be dropped back to third and dead and sunk, Part Tart A Too Tee fifth by a length and Googoo sixth and Stumble trailing the park, come on wham he'll come home straight to daddy and bring me home some honey and butter and stumblebum, now now I can see, can you see... *Man*, he'll make it at the far turn, it's still Wigwam that'll be, you know, down there, but boy when he comes on and that Ishmael start wailin' away boy, and comin' into the home stretch, and they'll be riding down through you'll hear their little sticks crackin' the rumps of those horses and the crowd roar... they'll come flashin' across that finish line, we'll collect our money... we'll—

BUCK: You and Manuel'll run to your little windows and collect your little pittances... and what are you gonna do with them, sit in haystack? Watch the airplaines?...

MILO: We'll be sittin' in a airstack and watch the hayplanes, and we'll get our money, and we won't even know what to do with it, huh! Fat chance we won't know what to do with it, fat chance *I* won't know what to do with it, I got *expenses*, boy, I got a family, I got a wife and four kids... And like you say we'll collect our pittance and we'll get back on that train and bring it back to New York... 'Cause boy, no matter what happens, everything that's gonna happen's *bound* to happen, and we're gonna have a *ball* – as long as you feel good in your *gut*... 'cause I *know*, the Lord is on my side.

MANUEL: I don't want a world like that from God.

BUCK: What do you mean?

MANUEL: That's what I mean, I don't want it. What a way to die!

BUCK: *Who's* dying?

MANUEL: All these creatures with their necks over barrels, mad people in here... If it's all the little doves'll die my eye would have opened a long time ago, I don't like it anyway, I don't *care*.

MILO: Manuel get your money out, we're gonna go place the bet now, the warning buzzer's ringing.

BUCK: Birds with long sharp knives that shine in the afternoon sun?

MANUEL: Yeah.

BUCK: And old Zing Twing Tong he lives up there in that pad and smokes opium of the world, opiums of Persia? All he's got is a mattress on the floor, a Travler portable radio, and he works, and his works under the mattress? Described as a wretched mean hovel in the *New York World Telegram*?

MANUEL: Ah Buck you're mad... I'm not gonna think about it, I'm going home and sleep after this, I don't wanta dream about wilted pigs and dead chickens in the barrel and horses and racetracks and no typewriter.

BUCK: You're right.

MANUEL: Besides it's a nowhere movie, we can't go see it, there's no monsters, all it is is a moon man with a suit on, I wanta see monstrous dinosaurs and mammals of the other world! Who wants to pay fifty thousand dollars to see guys with machines and panels and a girl in a monstrous lifebelt skirt! Let's cut out of here after the last race, I'm going *home*.

BUCK: All you gotta be, man, is a big sad cloud.

MANUEL: I just want classical angels... I don't wanta be a big sad cloud.

BUCK: Don't you wanta be a giant cloud, that's all I am, a giant cloud, leaning on its side, all vapours, yeah.

MANUEL: (*sadly*) I wish I was a giant cloud...

MILO: Come *on*, man, stop talking about giant clouds and let's go place those bets.

(MANUEL *and* MILO *rush off*.)

Act Three

(The scene is a living room of a ranch-style house, and in the door walks BUCK *and a new character called* IRWIN.)

IRWIN: What does Milo see in the Bishop?

BUCK: Well Milo was an altar boy when he was a kid you know, when his father was a bum in El Paso, he's just an old Jesuit, you know, actually... Besides you know what he does here in this house every night? He's interested in religion, he gets down on his knees with the kids and says the Lord's Prayer and puts them to bed. He really sweetens their cribs.

IRWIN: But I mean that Bishop isn't so much sharp, like we just heard his speech you know, Paul and I were standing in the back and we thought he was a pretty dull sort of ugh bore...

BUCK: Sure but it's his wife digs him more... Cora, you know.

IRWIN: Well, but Milo does too. All this mediocrity that's come later in our lives, when Milo was young and I was young and we kneeled on the dark Texas plain at night and vowed eternal holy friendship like – you know.

BUCK: Well as you say it all goes down the same hole.

IRWIN: Hum.

BUCK: Think Milo quieter now?

IRWIN: Well I guess he is, ah, but you know didn't I tell you how he came to my pad the other morning, I was playing my Bach Partitas and he started to roll sticks but at the same time he wanted to imitate the unaccompanied violinist but couldn't hardly get the tea out of his little box, when the violin screeched he'd throw up his arms wildly scraping bow on string, tried to lick the paper then the violin began an extended chaconne which left him thrashing on the floor scraping the bow wider and wider... (*laughs*)... spilt it...

BUCK: How *you* feeling?

IRWIN: I'm all right. I woke from a wine drunk two a.m. in the silence of the void birthday night, which I'd filled with "woes of the passing wind", the concluding lines of the mysterious Blake 'Crystal Cabinet', a poem I had never understood until that moment, like moaning he'd swelt in the crystal cabinet of the mind for years, but... you know, "another London there I saw". I can barely complete a straight line of thought, "when with ardour fierce and hands of flame I strove to seize the inmost form" and so on...

(*Enter* MILO *and* PAUL, *a new character*)

PAUL: Got television Milo?

MILO: Back room, back room m'boy, listen here daddies, the reason why I wanted to make such fast time back from the lecture *was* that I have a little bit of—

BUCK: You left the Bishop a mile down the road there—

MILO: —yes yes, 'bout *five* miles actually *was*, to turn you cats – you know, so as to dig everything, you know, straighten you out, like we're gonna have – like, I'm sick of hanging around here. What's that there you're doing there, what are you talking about there, boys?

IRWIN: I strove to seize the inmost form but burst the crystal cabinet and like a weeping babe became a weeping babe upon the wild—

MILO: Ah no more poetry for me.

(*Exeunt* MILO *and* PAUL)

IRWIN: Oh God.

BUCK: At least the Bishop is coming, huh?

IRWIN: Er, I don't think so, he looks dead.

BUCK: Do you like the way he lectures with his eyes closed?

IRWIN: Oh that's just a con routine to impress the women. Did you see all those awful middle-aged women sitting there, and old men retired under palm trees and the bullshit he said about astral bodies and auras, why doesn't he just take his clothes off and dance?

(*Enter* MILO'S *wife* CORA)

63

CORA: Where's Milo?

BUCK: Back room.

CORA: Milo!

MILO: (*off*) Yes darling!

(*Exit wife* CORA, *enter* MEZZ, *a guy who's wearing a bop cap, a real hepcat*)

MEZZ: What's all the action?

BUCK: Did you just get in in your M.G.?

MEZZ: Yeah man, it's outside. Milo said to be here at nine.

BUCK: Yeah you're just on time with everybody, s'great.

MEZZ: Well man, all I need is a little trip to the toilet, I'll be right back. Where's Milo?

BUCK: In the toilet.

(*Exit* MEZZ)

Do you know Mezz McGillicuddy, that guy? Used to be a radio announcer? He's an actor or sumpin'? Jumps on cars or sumpin'?

(*The door opens and in enters everybody, the* BISHOP, *the two aunts, and* BUCK *now on his high horse says:*)

Hello! We got here ahead of you!

(*Re-enter wife* CORA)

CORA: Won't you sit down, er, Mrs Bishop; why don't you sit on the couch here, and you Mrs Twidley? Er, ah, you can sit here, and can I bring you some coffee?

(*And the* BISHOP, *a good-looking guy in a black robe, says:*)

BISHOP: Why certainly, may I sit here?

CORA: Oh of course!... So, ah, let's all... yes.

BUCK: May I sit here on the floor beside you Bishop?

BISHOP: Why certainly! I see you... you are... you have been drinking a little, haven't you?

BUCK: Yes... sir... but I think that it's all right, I don't, er... we have things to talk about I guess, huh?

BISHOP: Yes I understand that you know something about Buddhism.

BUCK: Yes I do... but I don't know much about Krishna... I'm not too particularly interested, either, in Buddhism, actually.
(IRWIN *flops between the two old aunts who are sitting on the couch and says:*)

IRWIN: Well I'll sit here.

(*Re-enter the hepcat* MEZZ)

MEZZ: Well, ah, how d'you do? I'll sit over here, ah, how's everybody?

(*And* MILO *comes in,* PAUL *comes in, and they all sit down and the* BISHOP *in a great silence says:*)

BISHOP: *Well*!!

BUCK: Yeah!

CORA: Would you like something to drink Bishop? Water, Coca-Cola, coffee, tea?

BISHOP: No no thank you, I... I might have a cigarette.

BUCK: Bishop, (*handing him a cigarette*) I'm sure you won't mind if I follow my vice, (*drinking*) but I've already poured me a glass of white port hidden in the corner, s'why I wanted to sit here, I've been having a (*laughs*) hard day... I mean not really, I wanted to sit next to you and ask you a few questions. I wanted to ask you one specific question, do you believe that the universe is infinitely empty or do you think that there's a personal God and we all go back to heaven to perfection and bliss, that when God shows his face all our personalities'll vanish?

BISHOP: (*pleased*) Well yes, but there are *stages*.

IRWIN: How does one ascend the ladder of doves to heaven, the silver ladder of Moroccan doves to the great Sherifian* heaven?

BISHOP: Ah Mohammedan, Moroccan, Sherifian, step by step I think.

BUCK: Why do we have to take steps?... The stages... Do you agree with what I'm saying Mrs, ah Bishop, your aunt?...

AUNT 1: I, ah, I don't know anything about these things.

BUCK: You have a very nice nephew.

BISHOP: Yes.

MEZZ: Here's a cigarette – oh you *have* a cigarette already, I didn't mean to interrupt, I wanted to give you a cigarette.

BUCK: Cora also believes it has to be done in stages...

BISHOP: Well that's what I have been preaching, about stages, the bodhisattva stages, as you well know, being a Buddhist, or having read about it, involves *dhristi*... which is spiritual patience... We must no expect the grace of God so soon in a stage of impatience you see. Is needed, and also is needed *saha*,* zeal, *vitale*.*

BUCK: Yes.

BISHOP: And – precisely – which means we cannot expect salvation, or Nirvana, eh, if you wish to call it that, without making some ef-*fort* in the direction of God, some m o v e m e n t. (*And he twists.*)

IRWIN: Ooh, you twisted just like a snake then.

BISHOP: Yes?

IRWIN: Yes, your movement then was exactly like a super-natural illuminated serpent arching its back to heaven.

BISHOP: Well, yes, probably, of course.

IRWIN: I mean that was the *hippest* thing I've seen you do tonight.

BISHOP: Well, (*looking at* PAUL) who's *he*?

BUCK: Oh, that's Paul the saint.

BISHOP: Ah! Saint Who?

PAUL: Saint Paul.

BUCK: He's a Russian, you know.

BISHOP: Ah, a Russian! He has strange eyes and never says anything.

IRWIN: He's bashful.

BISHOP: Well Paul, what do *you* think?

PAUL: I don't know, I – I think everybody should love everybody, I think that's the only message... It's the only message and nobody ever believes it.

BISHOP: Well... and as I was saying there, about *vrykulata*, er, the steps towards the heart's desire, you are probably right.

BUCK: Isn't that the same as zeal, *vitale*?

BISHOP: Yes, but otherwise practising the ascensions of the stages it requires a great deal of...

IRWIN: Olives!

BISHOP: Olives, yes, that's nice. One falls into the danger of becoming *bhrasta*,* no-more-a-yogi, and *pramada** is upon us, and, which is cloudness of mind—

BUCK: The constant vision of God in all things and happenings including this moment will prevent us from worrying about cloudy downfalls?

BISHOP: Very wise!

BUCK: What do you think Bishop, am I speaking sense? Is it all right if I drink?

BISHOP: You're making sense and you do drink. (*laughter*)

IRWIN: (*to* BISHOP'S *first aunt*) Was he always like that as a little boy? Gee he must have been a strange little kid.

AUNT 1: Oh yes!

IRWIN: Do you mean... do you mind if I sit between you and your sister?

AUNT 1: Eh, of course not!

IRWIN: (*to the second aunt*) What *do you* have to say?

AUNT 2: I have nothing to say.

BISHOP: Well this is a strange and pleasant evening!... Let me add, *asagna* is not necessary, *asagna* is the cross-legged position, as our friend here. (BUCK *is sitting cross-legged on the floor.*)

BUCK: It's not really necessary, I know it's not really necessary, I just thought I would – I always sit like this at a good party.

BISHOP: Very good.

BUCK: And since I believe we're all in heaven now I see no reason to exercise discipline or worry about it... Would you shut the Gates of Paradise to those who... don't worry about it?

BISHOP: It's not in my power.

BUCK: Milo's wife Cora, do you realize the way she is?... she was in such a state of ecstasy the other day that when the children threw rotten eggs in her window she rejoiced in the opportunity God had given her to forgive?

BISHOP: Ah!

(*silence, long silence*)

BUCK: This is what Chekhov called the angel of silence, it just flew over us didn't it!

BISHOP: Ah yes... And this one here, he never says anything.

PAUL: Ah, well... djeva play baseball? (*Everybody laughs.*)

BISHOP: No, I'm afraid not.

PAUL: Did he ever take his clothes off with a girl?

IRWIN: I don't know, ask him... Somebody took their clothes off somewhere...

PAUL: Bishop I believe in taking clothes off... Do you?

BISHOP: Well, I see nothing wrong with that, of course. I think I'll have another cigarette now.

MILO: (*leaping up*) Any particular brand?

71

BISHOP: No no, anything.

BUCK: Well Bishop, what are we all doing here, and what strange days we live... isn't that so?

IRWIN: Yeah, I think we should all be ourselves sometime... soon as we can.

BISHOP: Yes but as to personal s-e-l-f, it is not something to become attached to as it gives rise to f a w l s e discriminations of the mundane.

IRWIN: The mundane's all we got... The surface, X, is all we got.

BISHOP: Yes but it was given to us by God and by God's omnipotent power—

MILO: Yes!

IRWIN: Well, how are you? (*to the second aunt now*)

AUNT 2: Fine thank you.

IRWIN: Er, are we making you unhappy?

AUNT 2: No not in the least

BISHOP: You're all very happy, or if not happy, have v e r v e, you're people with verve.

BUCK: Where'd you get that strange accent?

BISHOP: Well I'm from Czechoslovakia. I have to lecture tomorrow afternoon, I think I'd better be going very soon.

BUCK: Bishop, let me say, you're positively right in everything you say and you're a very sweet man.

BISHOP: My disciple here!

IRWIN: (*sings*) In the pines...

BISHOP: Oh he sings very well... You also sing? (*to* PAUL)

PAUL: I sing rock 'n' roll.

BISHOP: Oh can I hear you?

PAUL: Huh?

IRWIN: Go ahead Paul, sing, rock 'n' roll.

PAUL: Oh no, I don't want to sing... er... I'd rather talk, have you ever read Dostoevsky?

BISHOP: No.

PAUL: Do you dream? Djav any dreams?

BISHOP: Yes I dream...

PAUL: Can you tell me your latest dream?

BISHOP: Well, er, I guess it doesn't matter very much... my

dreams are not very important… I don't know. But I did have a dream last night but I'm not sure I can remember it…

PAUL: But you gotta remember it! All dreams are holy in the clasel halls of your hort!

BISHOP: I see.

PAUL: Grab everybody by the hands and kiss their hands.

IRWIN: You should see Paul take his clothes off.

BUCK: Ah shut up!

PAUL: Yeah yeah! Do you know about teenagers and how they wanta go to the moon, do you know about masturbation, did you ever walk down the street in the morning and rejoice in the little round asses of girls?

MILO: Erp.

CORA: Ur.

BISHOP: Well, so, a very strange confusion of ideas!

IRWIN: That was like Bela Lugosi that time… Do you think that everything is holy, Bishop?

BISHOP: As God's manifestations yes I think everything is holy.

PAUL: Did you read *The Idiot*?

BUCK: Hey Milo, we made it today, hey buddy, we made some money in the eighth race didn't we, we made some money finally in the eighth race!

IRWIN: Bishop, do you think holy flowers are holy? Do you think the world is holy?

BISHOP: Well yes, I think the world is... going to be holy.

IRWIN: Do you think the alligator is holy?

PAUL: And the hair is holy?

BUCK: Everything holy, Bishop?

IRWIN: Is the Bishop holy?

BUCK: Is Milo holy?

PAUL: Is Buck holy?

IRWIN: Is Paul holy?

BUCK: Is Irwin holy?

IRWIN: Is all holy?

BISHOP: I suppose. I would hope so.

IRWIN: Is Wow holy? I mean is Cora holy? Is holy holy? I mean are the streets holy? Is the ground holy?

BUCK: Is the racetrack holy? Is everything holy? Hooray for holy!

BISHOP: Well yes, I should imagine... but perhaps it may be that whatever you want, you'll get... But I really do think I'd better go now.

(*rising, and enter the little boy that is* MILO'S *littlest son*)

MILO: There's my little buddy there – what's the matter boy, did we wake you up with all that talk? Come on in here son and sit on your father's lap.

BISHOP: Ah, he has blond hair like his mother.

IRWIN: Child of light, child of light and gay delight.

BISHOP: Goodnight all of you, I think it's best to go now. I hope to see you all again soon, I hope you come hear my lectures and if you don't want to hear my lectures then at least we've been friends tonight...

BUCK: Goodnight... See you again... (*goodnights*)

(*They all exeunt, the* BISHOP, *the two old aunts, people leading them out the door and* BUCK *is sitting on the floor and says*:)

BUCK: The Bishop's all right. Ain't nothing wrong with the Bishop.

PAUL: What are we gonna do now, sleep?

BUCK: Well I'm going to sleep out in the yard in my sleeping bag and you sleep on the couch and Irwin sleep on that other couch and Milo's gonna go to bed and Mezz gonna drive back to the city but I'll put on some Symphony Sid* on the radio... Irwin do you think you – for a while, you know? – did you think you bugged his two aunts sittin' like that between 'em and all that holy avenues of the holy land and the terraces of the temple and all that stuff? How's things, is everything all right? (*he asks* MILO *as* MILO *comes back*)

MILO: Aw, the holy straight line of thought...

BUCK: I think we had a damn good talk. It's all right, Milo. Jesus Mezz McGillicuddy didn't say a word, that's what it's like to be well brought up.

MEZZ: Turn that up, man, give me some of that wine. Did I ever tell you show you my cowboy routine? Are they gone yet? Have they driven out the driveway?

MILO: (*looking out the window*) There they go now.

MEZZ: Well look—

MILO: Yass, how about some food around here, (*as* CORA *comes back through the door*) don't we have any f o o d around here?

BUCK: I'm not hungry.

IRWIN: *I* am! Want me to cook it?

MEZZ: —see, my cowboy routine, I come into this dusty old town in Arizona on my piebald pony and get off and go stompin' – turn on that radio louder man, that's great, Dizzy Gillespie man! – from the long ride from Flagstaff down to the desert, shake the dust off my hat, walk in the Four Star to slake my thirst, a bittermaker boiling maker maybe two three and there's Blackjack Slim at the end of the bar, "Wal Blackjack it's been a long time," I say and "It's certainly been," says he, "Mezz, how are things in Tombstone, I'm gonna put you right there now," so he's on the move, I see the twitch of his upper lip... twisting slightly to my left to give him a thinner profile I swing around and give him my Colt and blast blam blam! twice! For a moment... (BUCK *falls on the floor*) for a moment he leans on the bar as though he was ordering a shot and you hear his gun clatter on the floor, it was half out... Black Bart lies with his gun still stuck in his holster and beer drooling out of his lips.

BUCK: Let me do my cowboy!

IRWIN: Let me do one!

BUCK: All right you go first!

PAUL: I'll do my Russian cowboy—

IRWIN: —I come to the town, see, from the hills, there are some bushes, I open them real slow and I look and I'm a scissors sharpener and I dance with... and I look down and I peek, I put the bushes aside and I see what they're all doing down there in the town—

BUCK: Wait a minute! Wait a minute! I come riding in lookin' for my father's killers, I know they're in town; I walk across the dry boards of the sidewalk and my boots clomp and the long spur-jingle and push open the swingin' doors and there's Bart now, and his brothers and cousins on the side, they've all got their guns out and got me covered and they're all gonna blast me like they done my father...

MEZZ: What'd you do then?

BUCK: I turn into a ball of electricity and they all drop dead.

MILO: (*suddenly*) I'll tell you mine... Preacher ridin' into town, I'm standin' there at the bar with the preacher as he makes his sermon on the Lord quotin' chapter 26 verse 18 in the New Testament "Not a jot and a tittle verily shall ye know that was left"...* So there's a drunk in the corner drinkin' from his glass sittin' cross-legged on the floor drinkin' while the preacher makes his speech; I pull out my gun and aim it right at his head and say, "Don't you believe in G a w d?"... And I let him have it, right through the head.

BUCK: (*falls again*) Ugh!

MILO: All right you cats, I'm goin' to bed... We're all gettin' up at six a.m., five-forty-five really, and I'm going to drive you all back to the city. (*He leaves, exits.*)

IRWIN: That was strange.

PAUL: Where do we sleep tonight?

BUCK: I'll sleep outdoors in my bag, and you guys sleep in these couches... (*laughs*) I'm *dead*.

PAUL: You got another sleeping bag?

BUCK: Naw, I ain't got no other sleeping bag... you guys go to sleep... Why do you think that Milo shot me through the head after this long day that I spent with him... all the things he wanted me to do and all those bishops and everything, why did he do that?

IRWIN: Ah he was just demonstrating to you that you're a sinner and you're drinking from the Bishop's.........
....

BUCK: Well... I don't know. He had a big day, and he won in the eighth race and he made a little money, I should imagine he'd feel a little happy... but ah *hell*, I'm goin' back to the Coast, I'm goin' back to Frisco. I'm goin' out with this sleeping bag and you know why? When I wake up at 3 a.m. and I don't know where I am and I see all the stars above my sleep I realize what a vast bright room I'm in, the real room... I really sleep out there.

IRWIN: Any old room'll do.

BUCK: Yeah, but I'm goin'.

PAUL: (*curling up on the couch*) Hope I dream! Don't get

cold, Buck, wait a minute now come here Buckie, wait a minute now, goodnight brother, shake my hand, brother.

BUCK: Goodnight, brother Paul... goodnight, Saint Paul.

IRWIN: Goodnight, Buckie.

BUCK: Goodnight, Irwin... And I'm goin' out there, and you know what I got in my back pocket here, Milo's flute... then I'm going across that Holland Tunnel and get on the highway and hide my tail back west...

(BUCK *goes out.*)

PAUL: I'll take this blanket. You want this blanket?

IRWIN: No, I've got another one, turn the light off, I'm just gonna nod a little bit here, I'm tired.

PAUL: Me too...... What do you think about what happened tonight Irwin?

IRWIN: I don't know, I guess it doesn't matter... It was funny, I guess.

PAUL: Funny bishop huh?

IRWIN: Oh I was bored!

PAUL: When are we going back to New York – tomorrow?

IRWIN: Yeah we're going back with Milo at 5:45.

PAUL: Well I guess I'll sleep.

IRWIN: We gotta sleep some time.

PAUL: That's right Irwin me boy, I'm going to sleep now.

IRWIN: Milo's already asleep, I can hear him snoring.

PAUL: Shall I go in and jump in bed with his wife?

IRWIN: (laughs) No never mind... later.

PAUL: Buck's asleep now, ain't he?

IRWIN: No... listen. (*They hear a flute out in the yard.*) Buck's playing the flute under the stars.

PAUL: I wonder why.

IRWIN: Must be because... he's trying to figure out what all this is all about... whatever it's all about, you know... the world is what form is, and that's all you can say about it, huh?

PAUL: Yeah... I guess so. Let's have silent snores, huh? silent snores.

IRWIN: Okay.

(*Flute plays, curtain descends.*)

Note on the Text and Illustrations

The text of the present edition is based on the original un-edited 1957 typescript. Spelling and punctuation have been standardized, anglicized and made consistent throughout.

All pictures are reproduced with the kind permission of John Sampas, except for the photograph of Neal Cassady (reproduced with the permission of Corbis), the photographs of Lupine Road and Beaulieu Street (reproduced courtesy of Paul Maher Jr) and the photograph of the filming of *Pull My Daisy* (reproduced with the permission of John Cohen/Getty Images).

Notes

p. 16, *Aurobindo*: the Indian mystic, scholar, poet and philosopher Sri Aurobindo (1872–1950) wrote extensively in English.

p. 19, *Victrola*: An early phonograph.

p. 20, *Wee Small Hours*: A pioneering 1955 album by Frank Sinatra (1915–98).

p. 20, *Webcor three-speed box*: Webcor metal record centres were used for playing records of various rpms.

p. 27, *sweet potato*: 'Ocarina' (slang).

p. 46, *Dolgoruky*: Arkady Dolgoruky is the main character in *The Adolescent* (1875) – also translated as *The Raw Youth* – by Fyodor Dostoevsky (1821–81). The gambling referred to, however, probably comes from *The Gambler* by the same author; it seems Manuel has confused the two works (which have often been published together).

p. 56, *hog-head*: 'Locomotive driver' (US slang).

p. 67, *Sherifian*: A Moroccan religious dynasty.

p. 67, *saha*: "The earthly world of suffering" in Buddhist thought (derived from Sanskrit).

p. 67, *vitale*: "Vital" (French).

p. 69, *bhrasta*: "Lost, fallen" (derived from Sanskrit).

p. 69, *pramada*: "Negligence" (derived from Sanskrit).

p. 77, *Symphony Sid*: Sid "Symphony Sid" Torin (1909–84), the American jazz DJ, would have been very familiar to the jazz-obsessed Kerouac.

p. 79, *chapter 26 verse 18... was left*: The reference is incorrect: Milo probably means to refer to Matthew 5:18.

Extra Material

on

Jack Kerouac's

Beat Generation

Jack Kerouac's Life

Jack Kerouac was born Jean-Louis Kerouac on 12th March 1922, in the small industrial town of Lowell, Massachusetts. He had two elder siblings – a brother, Gerard (born 1916), and a sister, Caroline (born 1918). His parents were first-generation Catholic French-Canadian immigrants of Breton descent, and French was the language spoken at home during Kerouac's childhood. The family lived in an enclave of French Canadians, and he struggled with the English language when he first went to school. He remained bilingual all his life, and commentators have speculated whether the discursive and free flow of thought he developed in his later novels was in part a result of the fact that English was not his first language. He claimed in a letter that he modified the English language to suit the "French images" in his head. *Birth and Family Background*

His father Leo was a printer, and his mother Gabrielle, who outlived Jack, was a devout Catholic, and he imbibed from her a lifelong Catholic faith which he maintained to the end of his life, varied – although never replaced – only by a prolonged and intensive study of Buddhism in the 1950s. He also maintained a lifelong devotion to his mother – despite his image as a drug-addicted, alcoholic, roving free spirit – and he regularly returned home to be with her, and be looked after by her, after one of his hitch-hiking trips round America.

Even as a young child, Jack had begun writing short stories and drawing for illustrated comic books he and his friends produced on the lines of popular children's comics of the time. He also later wrote sports coverage for the Lowell newspaper, and a jazz column for his private school. He estimated that he had written over a million words by the time he was eighteen. *Early Life*

According to his novel *Visions of Gerard*, the semi-fictional account of this period of his life, Jack viewed his elder brother Gerard almost as a saint, who could communicate with angels. He was devastated when Gerard, who had always been ill with rheumatic fever, died at the age of nine, when Jack was four. Jack may have thought that he should have died in Gerard's place, seeing himself as less worthy, and it was perhaps then that he began to ponder the themes of death and suffering which were to permeate his works and thinking.

School   In his teens he progressed from his Catholic primary school on to Lowell High School. He had a strong athlete's build, and represented his school in American football, baseball and athletics. He was also extremely intelligent and diligent at his studies. He had at least one major romantic liaison – with Mary Carney, a fellow student of Irish descent (represented later in the novel *Maggie Cassidy* (1959)). The relationship did not last long, but Kerouac always wondered with some regret what would have happened if he had remained with her, married, and settled down to a happy and stable small-town life, going to church and barbecues with normal people. Yet Kerouac, with his talent, was already a candidate for university entrance, and also felt attracted to a bohemian big-city artist's life.

Literary Ambitions   A possible early influence on Kerouac's literary ambitions was a friend in Lowell, Sebastian Sampas, of Greek descent, who announced that he wished to be a literary figure, and encouraged Jack in similar aspirations. Together they read classics of American literature, such as the works of Thomas Wolfe and Walt Whitman, and discussed literary means of expression with each other. Kerouac was a voracious reader all his life, and among literally scores of British classic writers and literary characters whom he mentions in his correspondence and works are Blake, Coleridge, Joyce, Christopher Smart, Sherlock Holmes and Winnie the Pooh – at the same time, since he was bilingual, he could read French classic literature with ease, including the poetry of Baudelaire and Rimbaud. He also read works on literary criticism, philosophy and spirituality. Kerouac was devastated when Sampas was killed in March 1944 in the Allied landing at Anzio, and felt that a major link binding him with home had been broken.

University, the Navy and
Literary Friends   Jack, in order to prepare himself for entry to a prestigious university, had to spend a year in New York at the Horace Mann School. He finally entered Columbia University on a

scholarship received because he was a very promising American football player, and would star in the college team. However, by this time, war had broken out, and Jack interrupted his studies to serve in the merchant navy. On one of his sea trips, carrying bombs to Liverpool, he read John Galsworthy's *Forsyte Saga*, and it was then that he apparently first conceived the idea of producing just such a multi-volume saga woven from the events of his own life. He was in fact called up for training with the regular navy, but he forgot to call officers "sir", smoked on duty, and was found reading in the library when he should have been drilling. He was examined by psychiatrists, and was discharged from naval service allegedly because he had a "psychiatric disorder". Kerouac was prone to depression and mood swings, and it was at about this time that the first signs of the instability of character that was to lead to his later decline and early death began to become clearly apparent. Despite his talent and athletic physique, he was always very shy and withdrawn, and it is commonly speculated that one of the reasons for his decline into alcoholism and bitterness later in life was his inability to cope with being exposed to the public gaze after the success of his novel *On the Road* in 1957. He returned to New York in 1944, although due to injuries, including a broken leg, he never managed to achieve his original promise as an American football player or athlete. He began to attend poetry readings and literary gatherings, and started to acquire friends who would change his life, including his seventeen-year-old fellow student, the poet Allen Ginsberg. Ginsberg later wrote about their first meeting: "I remember being awed by him and amazed by him, because I'd never met a big jock who was intelligent and sensitive about poetry." They both desired to express, in different ways, their vision of a perfected America, and to achieve greatness in writing. Around this time too he met William S. Burroughs, the author of such later classics as *Junkie* and *Naked Lunch*.

Drawing their inspiration from, among others, Rimbaud and Dostoevsky, Kerouac and his new circle of friends began to be attracted by the lower reaches of society, which included spending whole nights in bars listening to jazz, which Jack felt drawn to and inspired by, drinking copiously and taking drugs. In August 1944, Jack was detained in prison as a significant witness to a murder, and it was at this point that he got married for the first time, to Edie Parker, a wealthy young socialite. Following the murder, the police, believing that Jack

Drink, Drugs, Marriage and Murder

might have important information, came looking for him in Edie's flat; his family either could not, or, because they disapproved of his new friends and interests, would not, come out with the $5,000 bail money, and so, possibly in order that her rich family would produce this money, Edie married Jack. He was let out of jail for a few hours for the marriage, one of the policemen acting as a witness. He and Edie had been together in a serious relationship for some time, so it was not purely a marriage of convenience. Nevertheless, they separated after just a couple of months, but remained good friends.

Jack had started using the stimulant Benzedrine regularly, enjoying the feeling of confidence it gave him. At the same time as living a dissolute life, Jack was under pressure from his parents to follow a conventional career and "straighten himself out". He staunchly defended himself, claiming that he was storing up experiences that he would use in his writing.

Death of Father   In 1946, Jack's father Leo died of cancer, and on his deathbed he enjoined Jack to take care of his mother, which he did faithfully throughout his life. From around this time to 1948, Kerouac had been engaged in writing his first published novel, *The Town and the City*, modelled in style on the novels of Thomas Wolfe.

Neal Cassady   It was also during this period that he first encountered Neal Cassady, who was to influence him greatly, becoming a major character, under various pseudonyms, in many of Jack's biographical novels. Neal had been in and out of reform schools, had stolen, according to him, over 500 cars for joyrides, and although he had very little formal education, he was intelligent and curious about life and its meaning. He had enormous energy, and was a refreshing change from the attitudinizing intellectuals and minor criminals whom Jack had been mixing with up till then, who all seemed to have a negative and depressing attitude to life; Jack saw Neal as "a wild yea-saying over-burst of American joy", almost a reversion to a much earlier period of American pioneering history.

It was from Cassady that Jack allegedly first received the inspiration for his "automatic prose", or "spontaneous writing", which he was to develop into a finely tuned means of expression in his later works. Jack received letters from Cassady in the early Fifties which were between 10,000 and 20,000 words long, or perhaps even longer. They were written almost as a stream-of-consciousness flow, with no linear structure, and consisting of a free association of thoughts with practically no punctuation. Kerouac derived from these letters the idea of a means of expression emerging straight from one's direct experience of life, and one's uncorrected thoughts, thrown straight down on paper. Many of his later works were written under the influence of Benzedrine on continuous rolls of paper, without page breaks or punctuation, over a period of just a few days during which he, driven by huge doses of these "bennies", would not sleep. Jack got the idea for the style of *On the Road* from Neal's letters, which he later described as "all first person, mad, confessional..."

The Town and the City, his first published work, was, how- *First Novel* ever, still written in a more conventional style; it first appeared in 1950, and received generally good reviews, though it did not sell well. Between this and his second published work, *On the Road* in 1957, Kerouac wrote at least a dozen more books of prose and poetry and reflections on the meaning of life, including examinations of Buddhist teaching. During this time, in order to gather material and try to become a successful writer, he embarked on his famous journeys across America, leading the "freewheeling" life which was later to become the popular conception of Kerouac and his friends; he also continued to frequent bohemian artistic circles in New York and San Francisco, becoming deeply knowledgeable about jazz.

At the same time he studied Buddhism extensively, attracted *Buddhism* by the central tenet that "all life is suffering". He was encouraged by the poet and Zen scholar Gary Snyder, and attempted living a monastic existence in the mountains, but ultimately found he didn't have the staying power. He also found many of his friends were unsympathetic to Buddhist ideas, and eventually he appeared to abandon the philosophy.

In November 1950, Jack got married for the second time, *Second Marriage* this time to a woman called Joan Haverty, who he had known for less than two months. She was bright, interested in the arts, but very shy and inhibited, and she could never afterwards say quite why she had married Jack. She did not get on with Jack's friends, and always felt that in Jack's life she was forced to take second place to his mother, who would criticize her for not looking after him properly. The couple separated soon after their marriage. When he left her, she was pregnant, and he immediately denied that he could be the father. He provided her with no financial support whatsoever, and when, in February 1952, she gave birth to a girl, Janet Michelle Kerouac, and sued him for maintenance, he had to be unearthed by police investigators. Jack again claimed that the girl couldn't possibly be his; however, he was so poor that apparently the judge refused to issue a maintenance order, since he wouldn't have been able to pay it anyway.

The daughter, who saw her father just twice during her entire life, was on heroin and LSD, funded by prostitution, by the time she was twelve, and had spells in numerous young offenders' institutions. She died in 1996, aged just forty-four.

Jack's instability during this period was becoming more and more apparent; he spent his time with semi-criminal characters such as Cassady, frequented bohemian circles, poetry readings and seedy jazz joints, was beginning to drink more and more heavily, and, in addition to overdoses of stimulants such as Benzedrine to help him stay awake and write, he was also experimenting with marijuana and morphine. However, re-membering his father's injunction to him to look after his mother, during the intervals of his dissipation he would return home to her, where she would generally cook and wash for him, treat him as her little boy, and forbid access to the house to what she saw as his unsuitable new friends, whether low-life or artistic. Friends of the time observed that for the very self-conscious Kerouac, it was only with his mother that he seemed to be completely himself, and to be able to behave naturally and spontaneously.

On the Road Throughout this entire period, he had been churning out millions of words mainly concerned with a narration of his own personal saga, and finally, in 1957, *On the Road* – a description of his freewheeling journeys across America, usually in Neal Cassady's company – was published. The novel fitted in with what was seen by young people as the new rebellious and freedom-seeking ethos of the time, demonstrated in music by the emergence of rock and roll in 1956, and embodied particularly by the young Elvis Presley and, in film, by such actors as James Dean and Marlon Brando. In Britain, this period saw the rise of the Angry Young Men, and rock singers with such names as Billy Fury and Marty Wilde – names invented to harmonize with what was seen to be the prevailing mood of youthful rebellion. The response of the press on both sides of the Atlantic ranged from amused contempt to horror at what was perceived as the undermining of traditional civilized values. *On the Road* was immediately seen as a trail-blazing representative work of this new generation. One review said that *On the Road* would be for the beat generation what Hemingway's *The Sun also Rises* had been for the lost generation.

Jack became an overnight celebrity, and was invited to appear on television shows and at book-signing receptions. There is general agreement that it was this fame that precipitated this complicated man's decline, for he could not handle being in the public gaze, but resorted to alcohol more and more in order to be able to cope with it. He invariably turned up on television or at literary receptions extremely drunk. *Fame*

Some commentators have claimed that Kerouac in fact invented the term "beat generation", and he had at one time thought of giving *On the Road* this title. However, general opinion is that it had emerged in bohemian artistic circles much earlier, and explanations have differed as to its meaning; some say it derived from the "beat" of free-flowing jazz, and signified the generation who lived in a completely untrammelled, carefree way, unplanned from moment to moment, like the improvisation of jazz. Others claimed that it meant "deadbeat" or down and out, and signified those people who had been hangovers from the Depression, or come back from the Second World War traumatized and unable to find or hold down jobs – those who frequently became tramps, alcoholics or mentally ill. Jack, in some of his Buddhist writing of 1954, tried to claim that the word "beat" contained an overtone of "beatific" or "beatitude" – i.e., the generation who through their "take no thought for the morrow" attitude to existence lived in a state of permanent spiritual grace. However, the term rapidly spun out of control; Burroughs commented acidly that the media had jumped on the bandwagon, and on the back of the "beat generation" and *On the Road* had sold a trillion Levi's and a million espresso coffee machines. However, just a short time later, the term "beatnik" was coined in the media to denote pejoratively the young people – mainly from wealthy backgrounds – who thought that the essence of being "beat" was not to wash or work, but to be permanently stoned on marijuana. Jack was horrified. He revealingly told an interviewer: *The "Beat Generation"*

> Do you know what a beatnik is?... they write a line of poetry, type it up in a great big expensive five-dollar binding book, put it under their arm, put on sandals, grow a little

goatee, walk down the street and say they're poets... It's just kind of a fad. It was invented by the press. Listen, I'm a railroad brakeman, merchant marine deckhand in wartime. Beatniks don't do those things. They don't want to work. They don't want to get jobs.

He later claimed that the fad had nothing to do with the "serious artists" who had started the whole thing. In an extraordinary declaration a year before his death, Kerouac said on a television programme:

> ...in the papers they called it "beat mutiny" and "beat insurrection", words I never used. Being a Catholic, I believe in order, tenderness and piety.

Kerouac's heavy drinking and outlandish behaviour lost him some of his old friends. At the same time, he saw the likes of Ginsberg and Burroughs being treated seriously in the media as writers and thinkers, while he was not, partly due to his habit of getting drunk before interviews and public appearances. Ginsberg and Burroughs engaged themselves publically in social issues from a liberal perspective, while Kerouac did not, preferring not to get involved in political debate. He disliked liberalism, privately seeing himself as an "American patriot".

Decline   In 1957, at the time of the publication of *On the Road*, he was still, despite his drinking and drug-taking, a handsome and fit man – but just a few years later, he was a shambling wreck, an alcoholic driven by his fame to the edge of mental breakdown, although he continued to write, and still appeared at poetry and literature events organized by Ginsberg and the rest of the circle, who were now moving away from Kerouac in their politics and ambitions.

Whenever he tried to isolate himself in forests or away from civilization to write, an overwhelming sense of loneliness overcame him, necessitating a swift return to places – principally large towns – where he could obtain his fix of companionship, alcohol, drugs and women.

Publishers were now, following the success of *On the Road*, asking for other manuscripts written by Kerouac in the past, and so, over the next few years, volume after volume was published, usually out of sequence of writing or story. There is a general agreement that the material written after about 1960 begins to show a great decline in power, as Kerouac descended into mental breakdown and alcoholism, including bouts of delirium tremens. The young handsome athletic "hipster" had now totally let his appearance go, and he was drinking as much as a quart of whiskey a day. He tried regularly going back to Lowell, to try to regain some stability in his old childhood haunts, but his former acquaintances were now pillars of the local establishment, and regularly felt impelled to throw this alcoholic out of their homes, or bar entry to him altogether. He was kicked out of numerous bars in the town, and once turned up for an interview on the local radio station blind drunk. His conversation even on literature and other cultural topics was disjointed and mundane. To provide some sort of excitement for himself, he would pick fights in bars and on the street for no reason.

He met Neal Cassady in 1964, but all understanding between them had been lost. Cassady was by now hanging out with Ken Kesey's group of itinerant early hippies in their psychedelically painted bus. Neal had moved on to the next generation, while Jack had been sidetracked and left behind.

On 19th September 1964, Jack's sister Caroline died of what *Death of Sister* was officially announced as a heart attack, but which was plausibly supposed by family and acquaintances to be suicide. This plunged him still further into depression. He had now almost completely lost touch with all his "beat generation" acquaintances.

In June 1965 he flew to Paris to try to research his French *Paris* ancestry. The visit was almost a total disaster as he was continually expelled from libraries and hotels for his drunk and disorderly behaviour.

In autumn 1966, Jack's mother suffered a stroke, which left *Mother's Illness and* her paralysed and bedridden, and in November of that year, *Third Marriage* to general surprise, Jack married Stella Sampas – the sister of his old acquaintance, Sebastian Sampas. She was totally conventional, and had never left Lowell – Jack may have been striving desperately to regain what he perceived as some Eden of his youth, before everything began to go wrong. He was at heart a traditionalist, hearkening back to an earlier period of American history; he desired a rural paradise where he could work on his own farm surrounded by friends. He was always extremely sympathetic to such peoples as the Native Americans, and to the peasants who he had seen on short trips to Mexico, because he saw in them the former spirit of American working people unspoilt by modern civilization. However, Jack may merely have married Stella because he wanted a nurse for his mother. He, Stella and his mother all lived together in Lowell, and the marriage lasted, with Stella nursing the mother back to partial recovery. She in fact outlived Jack by almost four years, dying in 1973.

Death of Cassady

In February 1968 came news that Neal Cassady had been found dead in Mexico of an overdose of drugs and alcohol. Jack at first refused to believe that this larger-than-life figure who had been so intimately bound up with his life and work had died, but when he finally did accept the truth, this break of the final link with the past pushed him still further into depression and isolation.

One of the last articles Kerouac wrote was an anti-communist, anti-hippy diatribe, and a journalist who tried to interview him at home in Lowell noted that, in spite of the fact that it was daytime, the curtains were drawn, and he was sitting hunched in front of a silent flickering television, smoking and drinking whiskey. There was no telephone; he said: "I don't have anyone to call, and nobody ever calls me." Kerouac claimed that he was now a strange solitary Catholic mystic, whose final plans were to have a hermitage in the woods, and write in old age, with "mellow hopes of Paradise (which comes to everybody anyway)".

Death and Funeral

On 21st October 1969, Kerouac died. He had been vomiting blood, and had been taken to hospital, where numerous blood transfusions were attempted. The cause of death was apparently intestinal haemorrhaging stemming from his alcoholism. He was buried at St Jean Baptiste Roman Catholic Church; the mourners included Stella Sampas, Ginsberg, Corso and Jack's family.

Posthumous Reputation

When he died, he had only $91 left. Most of his books, apart from *On The Road* and *Dharma Bums*, were out of print, and – despite such younger artists as Bob Dylan acknowledging that they had derived inspiration from him – in the eyes of the counter-culture he was a "lost leader", an angry young man who had turned reactionary. The first biography of him, by Ann Charters in 1974, reawakened interest, and Gerald Nicosia's massive biography of 1983 filled in some gaps. Other books then poured off the presses from acquaintances of Jack's such as Michael McClure and Carolyn Cassady, and volumes of his unpublished work were unearthed and issued. In 1995 the first edition of his letters appeared, edited by Ann Charters.

Now that the whole era can be seen historically and objectively, there has been a huge reawakening of interest in Kerouac and the beat generation, serving as the basis for intensive academic research, enabling the accretions of received opinion to be cleared away from Kerouac's persona and work, and for future generations to see him more clearly, not as a precursor or leader of any cultural trend, but as a complex individualist, with his own human contradictions and difficulties, and with his own very distinctive path in life.

Jack Kerouac's Works

Almost all of Kerouac's narrative works comprise a semi-fictionalized depiction of the current of his own life, usually with the major characters, including himself, given invented names. He had apparently been struck by the idea of turning his entire life into an epic multi-volume narrative as early as 1943, when he was a seaman on board an American naval vessel sailing to England.

Legend of Duluoz

He gave the overall narrative the title *Legend of Duluoz*; Duluoz was a Breton-Canadian name, like Kerouac, which the author adopted for his alter ego in a number of his novels retelling his life. However, the narrative was not written sequentially, and was certainly not published in any logical chronological order.

If the reader wishes to read the novels in a sequence which roughly corresponds to that of Kerouac's life, the following order may be suggested:

Visions of Gerard (written January 1956, published 1963), *Doctor Sax* (written July 1952, published 1959), *Maggie Cassidy* (written early 1953, published 1959), *The Town and the City* (written 1946–49, published 1950), *Vanity of Duluoz* (written 1968, published 1968), *On the Road* (written 1948–56, published 1957), *Visions of Cody* (written 1951–52, published 1959), *The Subterraneans* (written October 1953, published 1958), *Tristessa* (written 1955–56, published 1960), *The Dharma Bums* (written November 1957, published 1958), *Desolation Angels* (written 1956 and 1961, published 1965), *Big Sur* (written October 1961, published 1962), *Satori in Paris* (written 1965, published 1966).

The Town and the City   *The Town and the City* was Kerouac's first published work. It was written in a conventional, non-experimental prose style, and reviews, although praising its depth and breadth, pointed out that it was modelled to a large extent on previous writers such as Thomas Wolfe. It deals with the final few years of Kerouac's life in his home town of Lowell – from 1936 to 1939 – then his attendance at a private college in New York, followed by interrupted study at Columbia University, war service, first meetings with such artistic figures as Burroughs and Ginsberg, and his first encounters with Neal Cassady in early 1947. Kerouac adopts the pseudonym Peter Martin, while Ginsberg is called Leon Levinsky, and William Burroughs becomes Will Dennison.

On the Road   Written up from previous drafts in three weeks flat, *On the Road* begins to show signs of the "spontaneous flow of language", characterized by non-linear free association of ideas and lack of punctuation, which Kerouac was developing under the influence of Neal Cassady. The original manuscript of the novel had been written on one continuous roll of paper, and consisted of one 120-foot-long single-spaced paragraph with no punctuation. The version finally issued was heavily edited by the publisher. It details the events of 1946 to 1950, when Kerouac first met Cassady, and describes his trips through the country over the next four years in various vehicles, hitch-hiking and on trains, and gives loving descriptions of the American countryside, and of the people he met en route, such as tramps, alcoholics, drug addicts and decent poor working people; it also describes the kinds of work that Kerouac, Cassady and other similar acquaintances of theirs did to make a living. It was this book which first made Kerouac a household name, and engendered the myth of the carefree life of the open road, leading generations of future young people to take up the nomadic life for a short period, a trend which led indirectly to the beatniks, and ultimately, to the hippies of the late 60s. By the end of the novel, a mellow Kerouac seems to be now finally contemplating settling down and giving up his life on the open road. In this novel, Kerouac adopts the name Sal Paradise, Allen Ginsberg is Carlo Marx, William Burroughs is Old Bull Lee, and Neal Cassady becomes Dean Moriarty.

The Subterraneans   Written in three nights under the influence of Benzedrine, *The Subterraneans*, although set in San Francisco, relates to the summer of 1953 in New York. It tells the story of Kerouac's relationship with a drug-addicted young black girl, and how he re-established contact with other artistically inclined individuals who were still on the fringes of society at the time, such as Ginsberg and Corso. He was by now beginning to write entire long sections of his works in unpunctuated non-linear narrative, linked by free association – a style much more based on speech rhythms, or the improvisation and rhythm of jazz, than on conventional written English. Kerouac appears under the name of Leo Percepied.

The Dharma Bums relates to the period Kerouac spent on   *The Dharma Bums* the west coast from 1955 to 1956. This book was published shortly after *On the Road*, and remained in print throughout the Sixties and Seventies. It was, with the earlier novel, a major contributor to the developing ethos of the beatniks and, later, the hippies. Kerouac, as he had before, wrote the novel almost non-stop under the influence of Benzedrine; it details his time immersing himself in the Buddhist life. Kerouac goes under the name of Ray Smith, Gary Snyder becomes Japhy Ryder, and Ginsberg is called Alvah Goldbook. The novel portrays Smith and Ryder's journeying across the west coast of America, and into the mountains, to try to put their Buddhist beliefs into practice by hard manual labour, and by living in solitude, mainly on the heights of mountains. Japhy foresaw in this novel a "rucksack revolution", with millions of the present disaffected younger generation wandering round America with rucksacks, writing poetry, going up mountains to pray, showing compassion to all creatures, and transforming America into an Eden.

However, although Snyder/Ryder is dedicated, Smith occasionally finds himself unable to maintain the asceticism, and he rejoins the ordinary world for poetry-reading and bouts of wine-drinking and sex. The novel ends with him thankfully taking up a job alone in the mountains as a fire-watcher; at last he will be able to attempt to exist by himself to see whether he can really live out the ascetic ideal – an ordeal he could only stand for two months, as described in a journal he kept at the time (1956), which was later published as *Desolation Angels*.

Returning to the source material for *On the Road*, *Visions*   *Visions of Cody* *of Cody* describes in more detail the events of that novel, but continues them to 1952, giving a deeper insight into Neal Cassady's character. Cassady is referred to as Cody Pomeray in this novel.

Doctor Sax   *Doctor Sax* relates to the narrator's late childhood and early adolescence in Lowell – roughly 1930–36. Kerouac adopts here the name Duluoz, with the jocular adolescent abbreviation "Jackie".

Maggie Cassidy   Kerouac's adolescent romance with Mary Carney (the "Maggie Cassidy" of the title) provided the source for this novel, which goes back to the years 1938–39.

Tristessa   *Tristessa* deals with the period Kerouac spent in 1955–56 in Mexico City. "Tristessa" ("Sadness") is the literary pseudonym Kerouac gives to a gentle Mexican drug addict (real name "Esperanza" – "Hope") who Jack befriended in Mexico City. Tristessa, despite her drug addiction, funded by prostitution, is a devout Catholic; but moreover, with her gentleness and uncomplaining acceptance of her suffering, she displays what Kerouac thought of as a kind of instinctive Buddhism. Although in real life Kerouac did have some sexual contact with her towards the end of their acquaintanceship, in the book he is fascinated by her spiritual persona, and does not engage in any sexual relationship with her.

Big Sur   The events of summer 1961 in California, and the encroaching alcoholism following on the author's fame, form the substance of *Big Sur*. It describes one long self-destructive alcoholic binge, but at the same time Duluoz, Kerouac's alter ego here, emphasizes that the alcoholism is itself a by-product of his loss of belief in the perfectibility of humanity.

Visions of Gerard   *Visions of Gerard* deals with the first four years of Kerouac's childhood in Lowell, emphasizing his Catholic upbringing, and particularly the trauma he suffered when his elder brother Gerard died at the age of nine, when Jack himself was four. The brother is portrayed almost as a saint, who was revered by the nuns at his Catholic primary school, although this fictional brother declaims not only sentiments which would be pleasing to a Christian, but fragments from the teachings of Buddhism too.

Desolation Angels   *Desolation Angels* describes Kerouac's life between 1956–57 in Mexico, Virginia and New York. During the whole of this period Jack had kept a journal, and the entire book consists almost entirely of directly transcribed journal entries. It gives, in detail, the events of Jack's life in the period just before *On the Road*, through his meetings with Ginsberg, Snyder, Ferlinghetti and Corso, his discovery of Buddhism and his attempt to live the Buddhist life. Whereas *Dharma Bums* is much more a description of the external events of that period, *Desolation Angels* gives a deeper and more detailed account of the author's interior life at the time.

Satori in Paris narrates the events of the author's catastrophic journey to Paris in June 1965 to research his ancestry, when he was repeatedly thrown out of hotels and libraries for being drunk and disorderly, and succeeded in learning almost nothing. He spent nearly the entire time in a state of embittered loneliness. *Satori in Paris*

The final volume of Kerouac's semi-fictionalized autobiographical saga, *Vanity of Duluoz* goes back once more to the events of his late adolescence in Lowell, war service and return to New York. *Vanity of Duluoz*

Pic was written in 1969, and published in 1971. By the last year of his life the isolated and embittered writer had lost faith in the validity of the saga based on his own life, and so, working from an old manuscript, he attempted to write a novel seeing the world from another person's point of view – Pic, a young impoverished black boy. There is general agreement that this posthumously published novel, written during Kerouac's final alcoholic decline, shows a huge decline in ability, although it is interesting as being his only published non-Duluoz novel. *Pic*

Kerouac wrote copious quantities of poetry throughout his life, mainly in his free-flowing "spontaneous writing" style; most of it was published only posthumously. Among such major productions were *Mexico City Blues* (1959), *Poems all Sizes* (1992) and *Book of Haikus* (2003). *Poetry*

In autumn 1957, following the publication and excellent critical reception of *On the Road*, Kerouac had suddenly achieved fame and relative financial security. There was talk of a lucrative film deal of the novel, which never materialized, with Marlon Brando in the lead role; Jack, at this period of deep absorption in Buddhism, now wrote of possibly travelling round the world for the rest of his life trying to lead the life of an itinerant Buddhist monk seeking enlightenment. In September, New York "off-Broadway" director Leo Garin asked Kerouac for a play, and the author sat down and wrote it in one night, in the style of the "spontaneous flow of thoughts" and almost total absence of punctuation which he had now brought to a fine art. This style seemed naturally to be the ideal vehicle for creating a play. Throughout the play, Kerouac and his acquaintances, under fictionalized names, drink and gamble, and discuss the *Beat Generation* differing world views of Christianity – specifically Catholicism – Buddhism, and various "theosophical" ideas held by the Bishop, a character introduced in the third and final act, plus the spiritual ideas and teachings of Edgar Cayce, who Neal Cassady was fascinated by.

The first act takes place in the flat of "Julian Chauncey" in October 1955 – as we are informed rather clumsily a few seconds into the play. This Chauncey is presumed by commentators to be Al Sublette, a mulatto with a deep knowledge of the San Francisco jazz scene who Jack subsequently became close friends with. The small white man who enters later is a portrait of Charley Mew – Sublette's friend. They had both been seamen, and Jack had first met them when he had been hanging round various shipping offices in his days of casual work, looking for labour on board a ship; the character Milo is closest to Neal Cassady in personality.

The second act takes place at the races, where some of the friends, while still discussing the meaning of life, drink and gamble. The final act is set in Neal's house, and among other new characters introduced here are "the Bishop" and "Irwin"; Irwin was frequently the name given by Kerouac in his later works to Allen Ginsberg, and the Bishop was a bishop of the Liberal Catholic Church who Jack and Neal had come to know in 1956; Neal invited him to dinner at his house, and Kerouac, Ginsberg and other members of their set were present. The Liberal Catholic Church is in fact an offshoot of the Theosophical Society, believing in the unity of all religions, and members can, if they wish, give credence to the concepts of reincarnation and karma. The movement has more in common with Buddhist and spiritualist beliefs than with the orthodox Catholic Church.

The play was never performed in its entirety but seems to have lain on a warehouse shelf for years till it was rediscovered in late winter 2004.

However, in December 1958, Kerouac reworked the play by reading all the parts himself onto a tape recorder; although he took the underlying idea of whichever section he was reading, many speeches were spontaneously totally reworded to a background of jazz from the radio. A friend of Kerouac's, the artist and film director Al Leslie, later commented that, on hearing this, it struck him that all the characters in Jack's play were in fact aspects of Jack himself – which would certainly explain the complex interweaving of notions on Catholicism and Buddhism, and the high-spirited behaviour in the play.

Adaptations

Plans were made to improvise a film on the play, which was initially to be called *The Beat Generation*, but it was discovered that the name had already been copyrighted by MGM. It was to be interspersed with songs, and for this Ginsberg provided some of his own poems, which were set to music by Dave Amram. One of these, 'Pull My Daisy', which had been written over a period of years by both Ginsberg and Kerouac, was adopted as the film's title. The poets Ginsberg and Orlovsky were to play themselves, and Gregory Corso was to be Jack. The author himself taped a preliminary commentary. The film at first ran to over ninety minutes, but was finally reduced to half an hour, largely consisting, in black and white, of the third act of *Beat Generation* with musical sound-track by Amram, and song lyrics, as before, by Kerouac and Ginsberg; the actors speak their dialogue, but this part of the soundtrack is kept silent, while Jack incorporates yet another innovation – a spontaneous running narration throughout the film which he invented while listening on earphones to jazz. He describes what is happening, and introduces a voice-over lip synchronization for each character's words, adopting the appropriate accent and tone of voice.

Pull My Daisy has now become a cult fringe classic, and is regularly shown at film festivals. The script was published in 1961.

Select Bibliography

Biographies
Charters, Ann, *Kerouac: A Biography* (London: Deutsch 1974)
Charters, Ann, *The Portable Beat Reader* (London: Penguin,1992)
Maher, Paul, Jr *Kerouac: The Definitive Biography* (Lanham, MD: Taylor Trade, 2004)
Clark, Tom, *Jack Kerouac* (San Diego, CA: Harcourt Brace Jovanovich, 1984)
Miles, Barry, *Jack Kerouac, King of the Beats* (London: Virgin, 1998)

Nicosia, Gerald, *Memory Babe* (Berkeley, CA: University of California Press, 1994)
Turner, Steve, *Angelheaded Hipster* (London: Bloomsbury, 1996)

Additional Recommended Background Material

Cassady, Carolyn, *Off the Road: My Years with Cassady, Kerouac, and Ginsberg* (London: Flamingo, 1991)
Cook, Bruce, *The Beat Generation* (New York, NY: Scribner, 1971)
Hrebeniak, Michael, *Action Writing: Jack Kerouac's Wild Form* (Carbondale, IL: Southern Illinois University Press, 2006)
McClure, Michael, *Scratching the Beat Surface* (London: Penguin, 1994)
Phillips, Rod, *Forest Beatniks and Urban Thoreaus: Gary Snyder, Jack Kerouac, Lew Welch and Michael McClure* (New York, NY: Peter Lang, 2000)
Theado, Matt, *Understanding Jack Kerouac* (Columbia, SC: University of South Carolina Press, 2000)
Tytell, John, *Naked Angels: The Lives and Literature of the Beat Generation* (London: McGraw-Hill, 1976)

Film script
Pull My Daisy (1961)

Acknowledgements

The Publisher wishes to thank Brian Reeve for writing the apparatus and for his excellent editorial work, and David Amram, John Cohen, Paul Maher Jr and John Sampas for their assistance and for providing visual material. Special thanks to Caspian Dennis of the Abner Stein literary agency and Lisa Owens of the Wylie Agency for their support during the preparation of this book.

ONEWORLD CLASSICS

ONEWORLD CLASSICS aims to publish mainstream and lesser-known European classics in an innovative and striking way, while employing the highest editorial and production standards. By way of a unique approach the range offers much more, both visually and textually, than readers have come to expect from contemporary classics publishing.

∽

CHARLOTTE BRONTË: *Jane Eyre*

EMILY BRONTË: *Wuthering Heights*

ANTON CHEKHOV: *Sakhalin Island*
Translated by Brian Reeve

CHARLES DICKENS: *Great Expectations*

D.H. LAWRENCE: *The First Women in Love*
Unexpurgated Version

JAMES HANLEY: *Boy*

JANE AUSTEN: *Pride and Prejudice*

JANE AUSTEN: *Emma*

WILKIE COLLINS: *The Moonstone*

DESIDERIUS ERASMUS: *Praise of Folly* and
Pope Julius Barred from Heaven
Translated by Roger Clarke

GIUSEPPE GIOACCHINO BELLI: *Sonnets*
Translated by Mike Stocks

DANIEL DEFOE: *Robinson Crusoe*

ROBERT LOUIS STEVENSON: *Treasure Island*

MIKHAIL BULGAKOV: *Master and Margarita*
Translated by Hugh Aplin

GIACOMO LEOPARDI: *Canti*
Translated by J.G. Nichols

OSCAR WILDE: *The Picture of Dorian Gray*

D.H. LAWRENCE: *The Second Lady Chatterley's Lover*

GEOFFREY CHAUCER: *Canterbury Tales*
Adapted into modern English by Chris Lauer

HENRY MILLER: *Quiet Days in Clichy*

NATHANIEL HAWTHORNE: *The Scarlet Letter*

MARY WOLLSTONECRAFT SHELLEY: *Frankenstein*

FRANZ KAFKA: *Letter to My Father*
Translated by Hannah Stokes

To order any of our titles and for up-to-date information about our
current and forthcoming publications, please visit our website on:

www.oneworldclassics.com